A Brief History of
BELLE ISLE PLANTATION

Lancaster County
Virginia

1650–1782

Lonnie H. Lee

HERITAGE BOOKS
2020

HERITAGE BOOKS
AN IMPRINT OF HERITAGE BOOKS, INC.

Books, CDs, and more—Worldwide

For our listing of thousands of titles see our website
at
www.HeritageBooks.com

Published 2020 by
HERITAGE BOOKS, INC.
Publishing Division
5810 Ruatan Street
Berwyn Heights, Md. 20740

Copyright © 2020 Lonnie H. Lee

All rights reserved. No part of this book may be reproduced or transmitted in any form or by any means, electronic or mechanical, including photocopying, recording or by any information storage and retrieval system without written permission from the author, except for the inclusion of brief quotations in a review.

International Standard Book Number
Paperbound: 978-0-7884-5040-2

Dedication

This work is dedicated to the memory of those who lived and labored at *Belle Isle* during the colonial era—enslaved African Virginians, indentured servants, and members of the Powell, Kyrby, and Bertrand families—and to the Native Americans who were there long before. This brief history can do no more than scratch the surface of how these lives were shaped by a small neck of land on the Rappahannock River.

Contents

List of Maps and Illustrations	vii
Foreword	ix
Acknowledgments	xi
1 Native American Settlement	1
2 Thomas Powell and the Original *Belle Isle* Patent	7
3 Rawleigh Powell's Inheritance	17
4 John Bertrand and the Northern Neck Patent	27
5 Charlotte Jolly Bertrand and the Deep Creek Landing	41
6 The Mercantile Partnership of William and Mary Ann Bertrand	57
7 Thomas Bertrand Griffin and the *Belle Isle* Plantation House	79
8 Corbin Griffin and the End of *Belle Isle's* Bertrand Era	91
Appendix A: *Belle Isle* Plantation Timeline, 1650-1782	107
Appendix B: Family Trees	117
Bibliography	129
Annotated Index of Names	141

List of Maps and Illustrations

View of Mulberry Creek from *Belle Isle*
Photo by Marvin H. Lee, 2013
Courtesy, Anna Lee Holcomb and Robert Lee — xiii

Detail of *Virginia*, Captain John Smith, published 1624
Courtesy, Library of Congress, Geography and
 Map Division — 5

**Thomas Powell's 1650 Patent for 500 Acres on the
 Rappahannock River**
Courtesy, Library of Virginia, Richmond — 15

Detail of *Virginia and Maryland* . . .
Augustine Herrman and Thomas Withinbrook, 1673
Courtesy, Library of Congress, Geography and
 Map Division — 25

**Preamble to John Bertrand's 1698 Northern Neck Patent
 for 924 Acres on Deep Creek**
Courtesy, Library of Virginia, Richmond — 39

**Charlotte Bertrand's Codicil to John Bertrand's
 1701 Will**
Courtesy, Library of Virginia, Richmond — 55

Detail of *A New Map of Virginia, Mary-Land, and the improved parts of Pennsylvania...*
John Senex, 1719
Courtesy, Library of Congress Geography and
    Map Division   77

Detail of *A Map of the Most Inhabited Part of Virginia*
Joshua Fry and Peter Jefferson, 1755
Courtesy, Library of Congress Geography and
    Map Division   89

Paneled Entry and Stairwell of the 1767 *Belle Isle* Plantation House, 1935 Photo
Courtesy, the Winterthur Library: Winterthur Archives
    Wilmington, Delaware   105

***Belle Isle* Plantation House from a Civil War Era Sketch**
Courtesy, Mary Ball Washington Museum and Library,
    Lancaster, Virginia Historical Society   115

1660 Baptism Record of Charlotte Jolly Bertrand
Cozes Protestant Baptism Register
Courtesy, Archives Departmentales de la Charente-
    Maritime, I-43, La Rochelle, France   127

Foreword

This brief history seeks to identify and interpret the rich cache of surviving archival and primary records relating to the Virginia colonial plantation that came to be called *Belle Isle*. The abundant documentary evidence is enhanced by the preservation of this Lancaster County plantation by the Commonwealth of Virginia. In transactions consummated in 1992 and 2015, Virginia purchased virtually all of the land contained in the original 500-acre patent Thomas Powell filed in 1650 and the expanded 924-acre patent John Bertrand received from the Northern Neck Proprietary in 1698. From these acquisitions the Commonwealth has created Belle Isle State Park.

The William and Mary Center for Archeological Research has provided additional insight into the early history of the plantation through its 2003 and 2006 excavations at Belle Isle State Park.[1] Analyzing the findings of these excavations in

---

[1] William and Mary Center for Archeological Research, William H. Moore, David W. Lewes, and Joe B. Jones, *Archeological Evaluation of Sites 44LA147 and 44LA175, Belle Isle State Park, Lancaster County, Virginia* (Williamsburg, VA, 2006), 3-16.

the context of the large number of primary source records evaluated for this historical study makes it possible to draw significant conclusions about the colonial history of this Rappahannock River plantation.

Acknowledgments

This history of *Belle Isle* could not have been completed without the people and resources of Lancaster County, Virginia. I am especially grateful to the dedicated volunteers of the Lancaster, Virginia Historical Society and its Mary Ball Washington Library (Karen Hart, Executive Director). I owe a special debt of gratitude to the late Craig Kilby, a Lancaster-based researcher and published compiler of Virginia record abstracts and Carolyn Jett, genealogist and author of a superb history of Lancaster County, for their expert advice and guidance. I also want to thank representatives of other Lancaster institutions who have provided assistance: former Belle Isle State Park Manager Marceia Holland and current Park Manager Katherine Shepard, Robert Teagle of the Historic Christ Church Foundation, and Page Henley and Marcia Sitnik of St. Mary's Whitechapel Episcopal Church. I am also grateful for the assistance of knowledgable staff members in libraries and archives in the United States and Europe in which I conducted research for this book. Most of all, I am grateful for the support of my wife, Barbara, and friends and family who encouraged me to continue this research.

View of Mulberry Creek from *Belle Isle*
Photo by Marvin H. Lee, 2013
Courtesy, Anna Lee Holcomb and Robert Lee

1
Native American Settlement

The plantation that would eventually be known as *Belle Isle* had a long history as a Native American settlement. Archeological studies show evidence of nomadic human presence at this location during the Middle Archaic period (6500-3000 BC). By the Early Woodland period (beginning 1,000 BC), native tribes were building houses and forming villages along the river and the creeks that flow near the *Belle Isle*.

The seventeenth-century tribes living on the north shore of the Rappahannock River were part of the Powhatan group of Algonquin-speaking tribes. Their tribal name derives from the name of their primary chief—Powhatan. They consisted of thirty tribes speaking a common language, living between the fall line and the Atlantic Ocean extending north to the Potomac River and south to the present day North Carolina/Virginia line. The native settlements north of the Rappahannock River lived at the margin of the main body of tribes that owed tribute to Powhatan. This likely gave them some degree of independence from the great chief's control. The river and the Chesapeake Bay provided a rich variety of seafood—especially oysters, crabs, clams, and fish. They tended to live close to the river and their main supply of food.

Captain John Smith first visited this area in 1607 as the captive of Native Americans loyal to Powhatan. After gaining his freedom, Smith explored the Rappahannock River the following year looking for the "glistening metals" rumored to be in Virginia. While Smith did not find any such metal on this trip, he mapped this part of Virginia—documenting a series of Moraughtacund villages on the north bank of the Rappahannock containing about 300 people.[2] The map Smith published in 1624 shows a "Kings house" and other native buildings along Deep Creek at the plantation site.[3]

From 1634, Virginia colonial officials set aside the land between the Rappahannock and Potomac Rivers for Native Americans. It was called the Chicagoan Indian District. However, pressure quickly grew from English residents of

---

[2] Ibid., 3-4, and 17

[3] Captain John Smith and William Hole, *Virginia* (London, 1624) Map.

Virginia who wanted to move into the district.[4] The land between the rivers, later called the Northern Neck, was officially opened for English settlement with the formation of Northumberland County in 1648. Over the next two years some 15,000 European settlers are believed to have poured into the region. This massive migration and the rapid population growth it created led to the division of Northumberland that carved out Lancaster County in 1651.[5]

---

[4] Carolyn H. Jett, *Lancaster County, Virginia: Where the River Meets the Bay* (Lancaster, VA, 2003), 17-19, 32-35, 39.

[5] Robert A. Wheeler, *Lancaster County, Virginia, 1650-1750: The Evolution of a Southern Tidewater Community* (Brown University Phd. Dissertation, 1972), 14-16.

Detail of *Virginia*
Captain John Smith, Published 1624,
Courtesy, Library of Congress, Geography and Map Division
The map is roughly centered on the site of *Belle Isle* Plantation.

2
Thomas Powell's Original Belle Isle Patent, 1650-1670

Belle Isle was first patented just two years after English settlers were allowed to move into the Northern Neck. The plantation was located on a small neck of land protruding into the Rappahannock River bounded on the east by Deep Creek and on the west by Mulberry (sometimes called Mud) Creek. At the time of the original patent it was known as "Powell's Quarter," named for Thomas Powell (d. 1670)[6] who secured a 500-acre grant at this location on October 14, 1650.[7] Powell was part of the migration of settlers to the Rappahannock River basin from the Virginia counties of Isle of Wight, Nansemond, and Lower

---

[6] Neither this Thomas Powell nor his son Thomas Powell, Jr. should be confused with the Thomas Powell who married Mary Place, daughter of Francis Place, on September 30, 1666, in Old Rappahannock County; Robert K. Headley, *Married Well and Often: Marriages of the Northern Neck of Virginia, 1649-1800* (Baltimore, 2003), 287.

[7] Land Office Patents no. 2, 1643-1651, 288, Library of Virginia, Richmond.

Norfolk on the south side of the James River.[8] These settlers, many of whom were Puritans of various stripes, traveled by boat from the James River to the Chesapeake Bay and north to the Rappahannock River.[9] Some of them were able to register patents in 1650 on large tracts of the best riverfront land in what would become Lancaster County the following year. A Lancaster court fine of fifty pounds of tobacco levied against Thomas or his son of the same name for "swearing" in July of 1658 is an indication of the county's Puritan orientation.[10]

---

[8] The Thomas Powell who moved to Lancaster County had earlier patented 300 acres on the south side of the Nansemond River in 1637; Nell M. Nugent, *Cavaliers and Pioneers, A Calendar of Virginia Land Grants, 1623-1800* (Richmond, VA, 1934), vol. 1, 76. Thomas' brother, Howell Powell, also moved from Isle of Wight to Lancaster County, arriving by April 1654; William Lindsay Hopkins, *Isle of Wight County, Virginia Deeds, 1647-1710, Court Orders, 1693-1695, and Guardian Accounts, 1740-1767* (Athens, GA, 1993), 4; Ruth and Sam Sparacio, *Lancaster County Deed and Will Book, 1654-1661* (McLean, VA, 1991), 6.

[9] Brent Tarter, "Evidence of Religion in Seventeenth Century Virginia," in *From Jamestown to Jefferson: The Evolution of Religious Freedom in Virginia,* ed. Paul Rasor and Richard E. Bond (Charlottesville, VA, 2011), 30.

[10] Ruth and Sam Spararcio, *Lancaster County Order Book, 1656-1661* (McLean, VA, 1993), 33.

Powell used his Rappahannock River plantation along with 700 acres he patented on west side of the Corrotoman River in 1658[11] to rise to a position of prominence in Lancaster County. By the 1660s Powell was making extensive use of indentured servants and possibly some enslaved workers to command one of the larger labor forces in the county. The sixteen workers shown on Powell's 1663 tithable taxation record places him in the upper echelon of Lancaster planters that year. Tithable records of this type offer one of the best indicators of wealth among seventeenth-century Virginia settlers.[12] Powell's growing influence in Lancaster is confirmed by his selection by the colony's governor to be one of the elite planters chosen to

---

[11] Land Office Patents no. 4, 1655-1664, 223, Library of Virginia, Richmond. Powell probably controlled more acres in that area in partnership with his brother Howell. Records show they aggressively speculated with this land, finally selling a large tract in June of 1659; Sparacio, *Lancaster County Deed and Will Book, 1654-1661,* 12-13, 67-68, and 110; Beverley Fleet, *Virginia Colonial Abstracts* (Baltimore, 1961), vol. 1, 131 and 219; Nugent, *Cavaliers and Pioneers,* vol. 1, 360.

[12] Ibid., 39 and 96; Ruth and Sam Spararcio, *Lancaster County Order Book, 1662-1666* (McLean, VA, 1993), 31.

govern the county as court justices. He took the oath of office on August 25, 1659.[13]

Very little is known about Thomas Powell's first wife. In 1656, a neighbor accused Ann Powell of giving birth to a child who was not fathered by her husband. The Lancaster court ruled that this accusation was slanderous. The offending neighbor was sentenced to confess her sin before the congregation.[14] The accusation may have been triggered by Thomas Powell's foreclosure on 400 acres he previously sold this neighbor's husband.[15] Ann Powell died sometime between September of 1657 and October of 1664. Two of the Powell children, Thomas Jr. and Ann, were most likely products of this marriage.[16] The failure of Thomas Powell to name his daughter, Ann, in his will suggests he may have given credence to the accusation lodged against his wife alleging he was not her biological father.

---

[13] Sparacio, *Lancaster County Order Book, 1656-1661*, 50.

[14] Thomas Hoskins Warner, *History of Old Rappahannock County, 1656-1692* (Tappahannock, VA, 1965), 177; Ruth and Sam Sparacio, *Lancaster Deed and Will Book, 1654-1661* (McLean, VA, 1991), 12-13.

[15] Fleet, *Virginia Colonial Abstracts*, vol. 1, 120.

[16] Thomas Powell, Jr.'s appearance on the 1658 tithable list suggests he was born before 1642; Sparacio, *Lancaster County Order Book, 1656-1661*, 39.

In 1664, Thomas Powell filed a jointure for a marriage to Jane Catesby. The first documentation of Jane Catesby's presence in the colony is a head-right certificate issued by Lancaster County justices in January 1663 that lists her arriving in Lancaster with a group of immigrants that included indentured servants and enslaved persons. Jane's status is not specified in the immigration document.[17]

The provisions of the jointure issued by Thomas Powell appear exceedingly generous for that time and place. He promised Jane Catesby 200 pounds sterling and one-third of his 500-acre Rappahannock River plantation (to be paid at his death) to agree to the marriage. To set her mind at ease about the security of her position in this apparent May-December alliance, Powell put up a 500-pound sterling bond to guarantee that his heirs would not challenge the marriage agreement.

Unlike most Virginia pre-nuptial agreements of this period, this jointure makes no reference to Jane Catesby owning property prior to her marriage to Thomas Powell and does not include endorsements or signatures of men identified as her family members. While the agreement was signed by the

---

[17] Sparacio, *Lancaster County Order Book, 1662-1666*, 19.

prominent Lancaster County merchant, David Fox, the document does not indicate the nature of his relationship to Jane Catesby. Given his role in importing Jane into the colony, it is possible she was his relative or his servant. The details of the jointure between Thomas Powell and Jane Catesby strongly suggest that Thomas was an ardent groom pursuing a woman who was driving a very hard bargain.

The terms of the jointure also suggest that Thomas Powell had by 1664 become one of the wealthiest men in Lancaster County. The language of the agreement confirms that he was living at his Rappahannock River plantation in 1664. The agreement states that Jane Catesby's one-third share would be taken from Powell's "land lying and being on the North side of the Rappah River whereon I now live consisting of Five hundred acres being more or less."[18]

Powell's residence at his Rappahannock River plantation fourteen years after patenting it indicates that by then the well-to-do planter had probably built a substantial home by the rather modest Lancaster standards of the time. Archeological evidence

---

[18] Ruth and Sam Sparacio, *Lancaster County Deed and Will Book, 1661-1702* (McLean, VA, 1991), 42-43.

suggests Thomas Powell and his new bride lived on the western side of his 500-acre patent near Mulberry Creek where the earliest European artifacts have been recorded.[19]

---

[19] James River Institute for Archeology, Inc., *Phase I Archeological Survey of Belle Isle, Lancaster County, Virginia,* (Jamestown, VA, 1992), 54-55.

**Thomas Powell's 1650 Patent for 500 Acres
on the Rappahannock River**
Courtesy, Library of Virginia, Richmond

3
Rawleigh Powell's Inheritance, 1670-1692

About 1666, Jane Catesby Powell gave birth to Thomas Powell's new son and heir, Rawleigh. Thomas died four years after the birth of this son. Powell's will, probated on March 9, 1670, stipulated that his four-year-old son Rawleigh would inherit the entire estate.[20] The will designated Thomas' older son, Thomas, Jr., and John Gibson (apparently a nephew) to be co-executors of the estate and guardians of Rawleigh. Thomas Powell, Jr., who had already received substantial gifts from his father,[21] died the following year. The court then appointed a neighbor, Nathaniel Browne, to serve as co-executor and guardian. But Jane Catesby Powell had other ideas. On March 8, 1671, she was in Lancaster

---

[20] For the filing of Thomas Powell's will in Lancaster County, see *Lancaster County Order Book 1*, 141. The will was never recorded; Loose Wills, 104-105, Library of Virginia, Richmond. Craig M. Kilby graciously provided me with a copy of his abstract of this will.

[21] Sparacio, *Lancaster County Deed and Will Book, 1661-1702*, 62.

County Court with a new husband named John Kyrby (d. 1698). Lancaster records offer no clue to Kyrby's whereabouts prior to his marriage to Jane, but it is clear that she did not turn to one of Lancaster County's elite families for her new husband.

Jane Powell Kyrby produced for the court justices the jointure agreement with Thomas Powell and a deed for her portion of the plantation. The court immediately confirmed that the deed gave her rights to two-thirds of the plantation—one-third from the jointure and one-third as her lifetime interest as widow. The Kyrbys then moved to break the Thomas Powell will to give them the guardianship of young Rawleigh, control of the last third of the plantation, and responsibility for the other assets of the estate. While the court was initially reluctant to do this, it gave the Kyrbys what they wanted after the court-appointed executors/guardians withdrew after serving only one year.[22] The court also granted the Kyrbys the property of the deceased Thomas Powell Jr. after ruling he died intestate.[23]

---

[22] Ruth and Sam Sparacio, *Lancaster County Order Book, 1670-1674* (McLean, VA, 1993), 21 and 26.

[23] Ibid., 47-48.

While Jane Powell Kyrby does not appear in Lancaster County records after 1671, the birth of another son—Thomas Kyrby—is documented. The date of Jane's death is not known, but records indicate that she did not survive her sons or her second husband. In 1684, Rawleigh Powell filed a lawsuit against his stepfather that may have been intended to force John Kyrby to honor the provision of Thomas Powell's will that gave ownership of the plantation to Rawleigh on his eighteenth birthday rather than Virginia's statutory legal age of twenty-one. They apparently came to some agreement on the issue as the case was dropped.[24] Rawleigh died in 1687 as he reached the age of twenty-one. His will, assigned 300 acres of the plantation to his sister, Ann Dacres, and 200 acres to his stepfather, John Kyrby.[25] Ann was by then married to Charles Dacres, who served as minister of the North Farnham Parish at the time of his death in the spring of 1687.[26]

---

[24] Ruth and Sam Sparacio, *Lancaster County Order Book, 1682-1687* (McLean, VA, 1995), 50 and 52.

[25] Rawleigh Powell's will also identified Thomas Kyrby as his brother; *Lancaster County Will Book, vol. 5, 1674-1689*, 109.

[26] Ruth and Sam Sparacio, Old *Rappahannock County Order Books, 1685-1687* (McLean, VA, 1990), 81.

The language dividing *Powell's Quarter* in Rawleigh Powell's will reveals that there were at least two homes in different sections of the plantation in 1687—enabling the young man to establish an identity separate from his stepfather. At the time of his death Rawleigh was living at the lower or east end of the property where it was bounded by Deep Creek. This was the tract that he gave to his sister. He gave his stepfather the portion of the plantation on the upper or western side of the property where the earliest evidence of European activity has been recorded. It is likely that John Kyrby had always lived on this part of *Powell's Quarter*—perhaps in the original home of Thomas Powell that he had shared with Jane.[27] This arrangement of homes at the plantation is confirmed by Augustine Herrman's 1670 map of Virginia that marks three separate sites that may indicate building locations.[28] Both the description in Rawleigh's will and the visual presentation of the Herrman map depict a Rappahannock River plantation organized around scattered

---

[27] Rawleigh Powell's will was signed on February 6 and filed on March 9, 1687; *Lancaster County Will Book, vol. 5, 1674-1689,* 109; Sparacio, *Lancaster County Order Book, 1682-1687,* 106.

[28] Augustine Herrman and Thomas Withinbrook, *Virginia and Maryland as it is planted and inhabited this present year 1670* (London, 1673), Map.

dwellings rather than a single seat with dependencies radiating from it.

Rawleigh Powell's will gave John Kyrby a full ownership position in the plantation. Kyrby previously held a one-third life interest through his deceased wife, but he had no legal authority to sell any of it. The bequest of 200 acres from his stepson gave him a 40 percent position in the plantation and the legal right to sell his interest. By the fall of 1690, Ann Dacres had remarried[29] and sold her 300 acres to William Loyd of Old Rappahannock County (soon to be Richmond County). Loyd was a court justice and wealthy member of the North Farnham Parish Ann's previous husband had served.[30]

The following year, John Kyrby decided to give up his portion of the plantation, too. In November 1691, Kyrby purchased a plantation in Old Rappahannock (Richmond)

---

[29] After Charles Dacres' death, Ann Dacres married William Tomlyn and died before September 2, 1691; Ruth and Sam Sparacio, *Old Rappahannock County Order Book, 1689-1692* (McLean, VA, 1990), 19 and 71.

[30] In December 1690, William Loyd patented the 300 acres assigned by Rawleigh Powell to Ann Dacres; Fairfax Papers, BR Box 227 (2), folio 16, Huntington Library, San Marino, California.

County deferring most of the payment into 1692 and 1693.[31] In February 1692, he sold his 200 acres of *Powell's Quarter* to William Loyd's son John for 20,000 pounds of tobacco. Kirby was living in Richmond County when he died in 1698.[32] At the time of the 1692 sale of his portion of the plantation, John Kyrby had lived on and managed the plantation that would later be known as *Belle Isle* for more than twenty years.

Just before liquidating his share of *Powell's Quarter*, Kyrby paid a fine in a fornication judgement against Sarah Webb —one of his indentured servants. Sarah was convicted of having a child out of wedlock.[33] Such convictions were commonplace in Lancaster County in the late seventeenth century. A servant of Kyrby's close neighbor on Deep Creek, Nathaniel Browne, received a similar conviction about the same time. Female servants were not allowed to marry and were often the sexual targets of their masters or other men on the plantations where they worked. In most cases the women found guilty of fornication were required to compensate their masters for the

---

[31] Fleet, *Virginia Colonial Abstracts*, vol. 1, 260.

[32] *Lancaster County Deeds, Etc*, vol. 7, 1687-1700, 54.

[33] Ruth and Sam Sparacio, *Lancaster County Order Book, 1687-1691* (McLean, VA, 1995), 94.

fines the court imposed and the time they lost on the job by having at least six months added to their indenture contracts. Sometimes these women were punished by public whipping. Virginia plantations like *Powell's Quarter* continued to be heavily dependent on the labor of indentured servants throughout the seventeenth century.

Detail of *Virginia and Maryland* . . .
Augustine Herrman and Thomas Withinbrook, 1673
Courtesy, Library of Congress, Geography and Map Division
The site of the *Belle Isle* Plantation is slightly above and to the right of center.

4
John Bertrand and the Northern Neck Patent, 1692-1701

John Bertrand (c.1651-1701), French Huguenot refugee and Anglican clergyman, purchased *Powell's Quarter* (later called *Belle Isle*) in May 1692. Bertrand grew up the son of a Huguenot minister (Paul Bertrand) in the Protestant majority town of Cozes in the French Atlantic maritime province of Saintonge. John's grandfather (N. Bertrand) was also a Saintonge Protestant minister in the town of St-Jean d'Angle.[34] John Bertrand was educated and ordained for ministry in France, but recognizing that Louis XIV was preparing to outlaw Protestant worship in his realm, John immigrated to London in 1677. In England, John was re-ordained into the Anglican ministry[35] and served as

---

[34] For John Bertrand's father and grandfather in France, see Lonnie H. Lee, "The Transatlantic Legacy of the Protestant Church of Cozes," *The Huguenot Society Journal* 32 (2019), 38.

[35] John Bertrand Ordination Record #9535/3, Guildhall Library, London.

chaplain and tutor in the London home of a Huguenot nobleman.[36]

In 1686, John married Charlotte Jolly (1659-1721), another Huguenot exile in London. Charlotte, whose father was Charles Jolly (Sieur d'Esnaux), was from a prominent merchant/ noble family in Cozes.[37] John's mother (or step-mother), Marie Andre, and Charlotte's mother, Judith Andre, were cousins from the Andre family of merchants in Saintonge.[38] The Andres were,

---

[36] John Bertrand was listed as a minister member of the London household of Louis Casimir de la Rochefoucauld, Sieur de Fontruet; November 29, 1681, MR/R/R/032/08, London Metropolitan Archives.

[37] Charlotte's father, Charles Jolly, was a member of the Jolly de fie(f) et Chadignac family whose "noble house" was at St. Denis near Saintes. Charlotte's brother, Jean Jolly, was listed as Seigneur de Chadignac by 1692; Ch. Dangibeaud, Minutes de Notaires, C224, Archives Departmentales de la Charentes-Maritime La Rochelle [hereafter ADCMLR].

[38] Charlotte's maternal grandfather, Abraham Andre, was a merchant and Huguenot church elder in the village of Saujon, about eight miles from Cozes; Dangibeaud, *Minutes de Notaires,* C224, ADCMLR.

among other things, producing wine for export through La Rochelle to England and northern Europe.[39]

John and Charlotte left England with other Huguenot refugees (including relatives and friends from Cozes) and sailed for Virginia in the fall of 1687. They first lived near the North Farnham Church in Old Rappahannock County (present day Richmond County) where John served as minister of the parish.[40] In their first few years in the new world the couple had two children—William born in 1688 and Mary Ann born in 1690.[41]

The Huguenot exiles who migrated with the Bertrands settled along the Rappahannock River from Lancaster County north to Old Rappahannock (Richmond and Essex after 1692), Westmoreland, and Stafford Counties. When John took on a second parish assignment at St. Mary's Whitechapel in Lancaster County in 1690, he may well have been looking for a home that

---

[39] Information about the Bertrand and Jolly families in France is documented in the Cozes Protestant Baptism Register; 1-43, ADCMLR. For Andre family wine production, see Notaire Bargignac, 3E, 128/52, folio 143-144 and Notaire Tourneur, 3E, 26/1086, folio 244-245, ADCMLR.

[40] *Old Rappahannock County Order Book 2, 1686-1692*, 71-72.

[41] George Harrison Sanford King, Msslk5823a, Virginia Historical Society Library, Richmond.

was more accessible to both parishes. With the help of prominent North Farnham parishioners, William Loyd and his son John, the Bertrands acquired *Powell's Quarter*—a plantation that was more centrally located between the two churches he served (just across the Lancaster County line).[42]

Two years before purchasing the Lancaster County plantation, John had become the tutor of the sons of William Fitzhugh, a prominent Stafford County lawyer and planter. Fitzhugh had been planning to send his oldest son, William, to school in London because there were no adequate schools in Virginia. He changed his mind when he met John Bertrand. He wrote to a friend in London to describe how he unexpectedly discovered a way for his son to obtain a first rate education in Virginia:

> But accidentally meeting with a French Minister, a sober, learned, and discreet Gentleman, whom I persuaded to board and tutor him, which he had undertaken, in whose family there is nothing but French spoken which by continual Converse, will make him perfect in that tongue, and he takes great

---

[42] *Lancaster County Deed and Will Book 7, 1687-1700*, 56-57.

pains to teach him Latin, both which go on hitherto very well together...[43]

In his letter, Fitzhugh placed an order for books needed for his son's course of study under John Bertrand: three Latin grammars, three French common prayer books, and a French and Latin dictionary. He then wrote that the Huguenot minister/tutor had asked for a small buggy for ground transportation that would be "strong, plain, and light."[44] Fitzhugh compensated Bertrand by securing the buggy from England and making payments in pound sterling. The fees generated from tutoring provided a substantial boost to Bertrand's annual income as a clergyman.[45]

When John Bertrand moved to *Powell's Quarter* in 1692 his students (William Fitzhugh's sons and possibly other boys) went with him.[46] His role as tutor for the sons of the Fitzhugh

---

[43] Richard Beale Davis, ed., *William Fitzhugh and His Chesapeake World 1676-1701: The Fitzhugh Letters and Other Documents* (Chapel Hill, NC, 1963), 270-272.

[44] Ibid., 270-271. Fitzhugh acknowledged receipt of the French books in a letter to Nicholas Hayward dated July 14, 1692; Ibid., 290, 291, and 306.

[45] Ibid., 306, 313, and 318.

[46] Richard Beale Davis, *Intellectual life in the Colonial South, 1585-1763* (Knoxville, TN, 1978), 302.

family would continue until 1698 and include William's second son Henry. Fitzhugh reported in a 1698 letter that Henry was being boarded and very well educated by a minister who was a "most ingenious French gentleman." Fitzhugh went on to write that the only problem with this arrangement was the "unhealthfulness" of the Bertrand plantation where Henry was living. To cure the boy's "sickliness," Fitzhugh had decided to send him to London to continue his education.[47] Fitzhugh family records indicate Henry lived with the Bertrands from 1689 to 1697 (from age three to age eleven). His last five years with his Huguenot tutor would have been in the unhealthful living conditions of *Powell's Quarter*. The adult Henry Fitzhugh was considered to be a distinguished scholar who also served in a governance role for the county and the colony at large.[48]

The Bertrand/Fitzhugh connection would prove to be decisive in the history of *Belle Isle*. Through John and Charlotte's relatives and friends from the Protestant Church of

---

[47] Davis, ed., *William Fitzhugh and his Chesapeake World, 1676-1701*, 361.

[48] Stuart E. Brown, Jr., *Annals of Clarke County, Virginia* (Berryville, VA, 1983), 226-236; George Harrison Sanford King, *The Register of Overwharton Parish, Stafford County, Virginia, 1723-1758, and Sundry Historical and Genealogical Notes* (Fredericksburg, VA, 1961), 224-225.

Cozes in western France, they had relationships with Huguenot merchants in La Rochelle, London, Boston, New York City, and the West Indies.[49] Hoping to use these personal connections to build their own mercantile and trading business, they set out to develop a landing for transatlantic ships on their property where Deep Creek flows into the Rappahannock River.[50] Deep Creek was deep enough and protected enough to accommodate ocean going vessels of the time, but the 500 acres contained in Thomas Powell's original patent did not give the Bertrands enough of the creek's shoreline to build the facilities they needed. There was, however, more than enough surplus land that had never been patented extending north from *Powell's Quarter* to the head of Deep Creek.

---

[49] John and Charlotte Bertrand's relationships with relatives and friends across the Atlantic world are documented in Lee, "The Transatlantic Legacy of the Protestant Church of Coze," 36-39, and 51-54.

[50] For the importance of relationships of kinship and trust among seventeenth-century merchants, see J. F. Bosher, "Huguenot Merchants and the Protestant International in the Seventeenth Century," *The William and Mary Quarterly* 52 (January 1995), 77-102 and April Lee Hatfield, *Atlantic Virginia: Intercolonial Relationships in the Seventeenth Century* (Philadelphia, 2004).

John and Charlotte set out to acquire or control this adjacent land. To achieve their goal, they allied themselves with William Fitzhugh, who was by 1693 one of two Virginia agents of the Northern Neck Proprietary that Charles II had created to reward some of his supporters. The King had made these supporters the "Lords Proprietors" and "barons" of the region of Virginia between the Rappahannock and Potomac Rivers, with the right to grant land and tax land owners.[51] The Bertrands' initial effort to secure possession of this Deep Creek property (possibly through a deed issued by Fitzhugh) was thwarted by the Lancaster County Court. Its leading justice, Robert Carter, was locked in a bitter struggle with William Fitzhugh at this time over the legal authority of the Northern Neck Proprietary to issue land patents and tax landowners in this region of Virginia. After a bitter and complicated court battle, the Lancaster justices ruled against the Bertrands' claim on the Deep Creek surplus land. In

---

[51] Charles II established the Northern Neck Proprietary during his exile in France in 1649; Douglas Southall Freeman, *Young Washington*, vol. 1, Appendix I-1, 447-513.

March of 1694, the Lancaster County Court assigned most of this land to one of John and Charlotte's neighbors.[52]

But four years later, the tide turned in the long struggle between Fitzhugh and "King" Carter. The Northern Neck Proprietary decisively prevailed against the powerful landowners and colonial officials who opposed its authority.[53] With its legal standing firmly established, the Proprietary overturned the 1694 Lancaster Court ruling and issued a new patent that assigned virtually all of the disputed land to John Bertrand—enlarging his Rappahannock plantation from 500 acres to 924 acres. This new patent (initialed by William Fitzhugh) included the entire western shoreline of Deep Creek—giving the Bertrands the perfect setting to develop a landing for intercolonial and transatlantic trading operations. It is also significant that the additional acres provided by the 1698 patent includes the site for

---

[52] Ruth and Sam Sparacio, *Lancaster County Order Book, 1691-1695* (McLean, VA, 1995), 70-71.

[53] Davis, ed., *William Fitzhugh and His Chesapeake World*, 39-46.

the 1767 Belle Isle plantation house (built by John Bertrand's great grandson) that survives to the present day.[54]

With a new patent for a much larger plantation, John Bertrand moved quickly to increase his labor force to eleven workers in 1700.[55] During his lifetime the plantation used a mixture of indentured servants and enslaved African Virginians, with servants forming the majority.[56] Working and living conditions for servants and enslaved workers at Lancaster's plantations were exceedingly difficult and mortality rates were high. Masters in English America had far more control over their servants than was the case in England. The Virginia indenture

---

[54] Northern Neck Grants, no. 2, 1694-1700, 293-295, Library of Virginia, Richmond.

[55] Ruth and Sam Sparacio, *Lancaster County Order Book, 1699-1701* (McLean, VA, 1998), 32 and 84.

[56] Documented indentured servants of John Bertrand include William Lawson, Thomas Whitaker, William Stephenson, Bryon Muchleroy, John Howell, Eleanor Deinne, Owen Lord, Thomas Roberts, Jeffrey Brassier, and Robert Furney. Bertrand named three African Virginian enslaved women in his will—Sue, Katy, and Doly—who he bequeathed to his daughter Mary Ann. Other enslaved persons identified with John Bertrand in county records include eight-year-old Peter and six-year-old John in 1690 and the runaways Jack and Tom in 1700.

contracts stipulated that planters could house, feed, and discipline their servants according to the "custom of the country," a major loophole giving them wide latitude to do as they pleased.[57]

John Bertrand, like other plantation owners of this period, was frequently in court to deal with incidents of theft, absenteeism, and rebellion among indentured servants. In one case, three of Bertrand's servants were found guilty of killing two hogs. Virginia planters typically branded their hogs and let them run loose in the woods. While servants could legally kill unbranded wild hogs to augment their diets, in this case they apparently killed hogs that belonged to a neighbor or business associate of John Bertrand. Two of the servants were fined and assigned two additional years of service because they could not pay their fines. The third servant, Eleanor Deinne, chose another way to pay her fine. She elected to receive twenty lashes for every 500 pounds of tobacco that she owed. For her, the whip was preferable to extending her time as a servant.[58]

---

[57] James Horn, *Adapting to a New World: English Society in the Seventeenth-Century Chesapeake* (Chapel Hill, NC, 1994), 266-274.

[58] Sparacio, *Lancaster County Order Book, 1699-1701*, 14-15.

In the summer of 1701, fourteen years after arriving in Virginia and nine years after purchasing his Rappahannock River plantation, John Bertrand died and was likely buried on his plantation.[59] While he made an important contribution to the colony as an Anglican clergyman,[60] the leader of a significant Huguenot migration, and a pioneer educator, John Bertrand's influence on *Belle Isle* plantation was transformative. His expansion of its acreage to include the entire western shoreline of Deep Creek made possible the plantation's future role as one of the intercolonial and transatlantic trading centers of the Rappahannock region. John Bertrand laid the groundwork for his children and grandchildren to become respected members of the Lancaster gentry.

---

[59] In an early twentieth-century essay on the history of St. Mary's Whitechapel Church, Elizabeth Lewis Neale wrote that John Bertrand was buried on his plantation at *Belle Isle*; Elizabeth Lewis Neal, "St. Mary's Whitechapel, Lancaster, Virginia," in *Colonial Churches: A Series of Sketches of Churches in the Original Colony of Virginia*, ed. *W. M. Clarke* (Richmond, VA, 1907), 308-312. Early colonial graves at Belle Isle State Park may be hidden by an overgrown grove of trees in an area long identified as the "graveyard field."

[60] County records suggest that Bertrand served North Farnham Parish from 1687 to 1693 and again from about 1698 until his death in 1701, and St. Mary's Whitechapel Parish from 1690 until 1698.

Preamble to John Bertrand's 1698 Northern Neck Patent for 924 Acres on Deep Creek

The Initials of Proprietary Agents William Fitzhugh and George Brent are in the Upper Right Corner.

Courtesy, Library of Virginia, Richmond

5
Charlotte Jolly Bertrand and the Deep Creek Landing, 1701-1713

At the death of John Bertrand in 1701, his wife, Charlotte, assumed management of their Rappahannock River plantation. John's will left the plantation to his thirteen-year-old son, William, but named Charlotte the sole executor and administrator of his estate.[61] This gave her legal standing to run the plantation and its related businesses in Virginia's patriarchal legal system. Charlotte subsequently launched a career as an independent business woman in Virginia that few English colonial women were capable of performing. Widows in colonial Virginia were subject to strong social and legal pressures to remarry and to relinquish the ownership of their plantations to their new husbands. The courts usually required widows to have their children adopted by their next husband through the indentured servant contracts that were commonly used for this

---

[61] John Bertrand's will was dated December 26, 1700, and probated on September 10, 1701; *Lancaster County Will Book 8, 1690-1709*, 105-105a.

purpose. Though she was forty-one years old with a thirteen-year-old son, an eleven-year-old daughter, and a 924-acre plantation to manage, Charlotte chose not to play by the rules that Virginia typically imposed on widows. She proved resourceful enough to fend off the admonitions of parish and county officials as she followed her own vision for the future of her family in the new world.

John Bertrand's will followed English tradition and the usual practice of the French nobility by leaving the entire plantation to his first and only son, William. But the provision naming his daughter, Mary Ann, as next in line to inherit the plantation (ahead of Paul Bertrand III—John's nephew in London) was a striking departure from the English practice of primogeniture and more in line with the inheritance customs of merchants in Saintonge.[62] In another nod to Saintonge inheritance customs, the will assigns to Mary Ann a full share of the personal property of the estate. Once again following English tradition, the language of the will entailed the plantation. Entailment meant the beneficiary had a limited form of ownership and could not sell, mortgage, or bequeath the

---

[62] Paula Wheeler Carlo, *Huguenot Refugees in Colonial New York: Becoming American in the Hudson Valley* (Brighton, UK, 2005), 147-148.

plantation outside the family. By keeping the plantation in tact and designating it a permanent legacy to be passed on to the next family member inheriting, John Bertrand was seeking to make it the centerpiece of the family's Virginia identity for centuries to come.

By Virginia statute, Charlotte would have a life interest in one-third of the plantation. At her death this portion of the plantation would go to William or, if he were deceased, to the next person in line to inherit. The will assigned to Mary Ann three enslaved women. The additional enslaved workers not named in the will were considered real property to be passed on to William with the plantation.[63] In the event Charlotte died before the children were of age, the will designated the Bertrands' close friend and Cozes Huguenot emigre, James Foushee, to assume responsibility for the children and the estate.

When Charlotte Bertrand submitted the will of her husband to be proved in Lancaster County Court, she chose not

---

[63] For an explanation of the status of enslaved persons as real property under Virginia law, see Craig Kilby, "Did You Know Slaves Were Real Property," Mary Ball Washington History and Research Center Newsletter 1, issue 2, (November 2015).

to do so in person. Instead, she sent a hand-written note to the justices. The note was copied into the court record as follows:

> To the Worshipful Court of Lancaster,
>
> Gentlemen, These are to acqt. You that last night I did intend by God's help to bee att Court this day to have waited on ye Worships in ordr: to have my husbands Will proved, but I am taken very ill, but hoping that yr: worships wont take it ill, I have for that reason sent my Dear Husbands Will by Mr. Charles Dobson to be proved before ye worships. I therefore humbly beg of yr: worships to admit it to be proved and I shall as in duty bound ever pray for yr. worships welfare: Charlotte Bertrand.[64]

This note reveals that Charlotte was proficient in her second language and in the social graces expected of an aristocratic woman. Her note skillfully projects the respectful image she wanted to convey to the justices and shows her understanding of the patriarchal culture in which she lived. The Lancaster record trail of her activities from 1701 to 1713 shows that Charlotte's education and business competency were well beyond most women in colonial Virginia. Moreover, Charlotte's documented

---

[64] *Lancaster County Will Book 8, 1690-1709*, 105.

activities clearly demonstrate her willingness to break through the limitations Virginia had established for her gender.

Charlotte's interest in running *Belle Isle* and developing its potential for intercolonial and international trade emerged from her cultural background on the west coast of France. Women from merchant families in Saintonge commonly worked along side their husbands. Charlotte's mother, Judith Andre, was actively engaged in her family's wine production business in Saintonge. A French record shows her signature on a contract to sell vine cuttings to another merchant in 1690.[65] Since this was a role English women were not encouraged (and perhaps not permitted) to pursue in early eighteenth-century Virginia, an English husband would have been unlikely to understand or support Charlotte's enthusiasm for directing the business operations of the Bertrand plantation.

One of the challenges Charlotte faced in running the plantation was managing its labor force that included indentured servants and enslaved African Virginians. While Charlotte was not in court as frequently as her husband had been to address the plantation's labor problems, she was creative in her efforts to

---

[65] Notaire Tourneur, 3E, 26/1086, folio 244-245, ADCMLR.

address them. Records reveal that she signed an unusual indenture contract in 1707. Charlotte promised to provide food and medical care for one servant (also the mother of two other servants) in exchange for the woman's commitment to spin the wool produced by all of the plantation's sheep.[66] While Charlotte continued to employ indentured servants for the Bertrand plantation, she also began the transition to a labor force that was mostly enslaved African Virginians.[67]

Another difficult challenge for Charlotte was meeting the terms under which her husband purchased the plantation from John Loyd. Because the Bertrands did not have the 200 pounds sterling purchase price, they took out a mortgage with the seller to be repaid in cash. In 1696, four years after taking possession of the plantation, the Bertrands still owed 134 pounds sterling. John's salary as a minister was paid in tobacco and the price of this commodity had plummeted in the years following his agreement with John Loyd—making it much more difficult for the Bertrands to make their payments in cash. In September

---

[66] Ruth and Sam Sparacio, *Lancaster County Deed Book, 1706-1710* (McLean, VA, 1995), 13-14.

[67] Servants listed in the records during Charlotte's tenure are Robert Tenney, Frances Pore, and her children Alexander Pore and Eleanor Pore.

1703, two years after John's death, John Loyd was suing Charlotte for the sixty-six pounds sterling she still owed him. Without John's salary as a minister or his income as a tutor Charlotte had to find a way to pay the mortgage and put the plantation on a sound financial footing.[68]

Lancaster records suggest the Bertrands had completed their landing for transatlantic ships by 1701 and were engaged in business as merchants. Charlotte made the landing a trans-shipment point for tobacco headed for England and a dock on which to unload imported European manufactured goods for sale to Virginia settlers.[69] On April 8, 1702, the Lancaster County Court directed that a chest of goods ordered by John Steptoe be put up for auction to settle his estate. Steptoe died before picking up the order that had been shipped from England to the Bertrand landing. Most of the goods in the chest were European fabrics that Charlotte apparently believed had been ordered by her

---

[68] Ruth and Sam Sparacio, *Lancaster County Order Book, 1695-1699* (McLean, VA, 1995), 27, 43, 44, 46, and 47; *Lancaster County Order Book 5, 1702-1713*, 18.

[69] William Waller Hening, ed., *Statutes at Large: Being a Collection of All the Laws of Virginia* (New York, 1821), vol. 6, 173. *Lancaster Order Book 7, 1721-1729*, 65.

husband before his death to be sold through the Bertrand "store." When the court justices ruled that this chest had been ordered and paid for by Steptoe, they directed Charlotte to return the goods she had already removed from the chest and to account for them. She subsequently purchased some of the fabrics at an auction managed by a Lancaster merchant named William Fox.

Some months after the contents of the chest had been auctioned, Charlotte was taken to court by the English merchant who shipped them to Virginia. The merchant's lawyer submitted evidence to the court that the late John Bertrand was the retailer for these goods, just as Charlotte had believed in the beginning. The English merchant had not been paid and was suing the Bertrand estate for the bill.[70] On January 14, 1703, the court found Charlotte liable for 26 pounds sterling on this chest of goods. Charlotte then went to court to sue William Fox for removing merchandise she could have sold at a substantial profit. On September 9, 1703, the justices agreed with Charlotte, awarding her fifty-two pounds sterling—giving her a substantial mark-up on the merchandise. By filing this suit Charlotte took on

---

[70] *Lancaster Order Book 5, 1702-1713*, 110-111.

and prevailed against one of the wealthiest men in the county who also happened to be one of the Lancaster court justices.[71]

Another sign of Charlotte's merchant activities was her large number of business transactions recorded in the Lancaster County records after 1700. The nature of most of the transactions are not revealed by the court record—only that one party was looking to collect payment from the other. But some of these law suits show that Charlotte was engaged in the work of a local merchant. On October 13, 1703, Charlotte sued William Fox for five pounds and twenty shillings for goods she had delivered to him.[72] It is probably not a coincidence that the 1736 estate inventory of Charlotte's son-in-law included money scales for a store and the 1761 inventory of her son refers to a building on the plantation called the "store" that contained two pairs of weights and scales.[73]

Seventeenth-century stores in Virginia usually offered a wide variety of goods—fabrics, clothing, shoes, gloves, hats,

---

[71] Ibid., 18, 44, and 45. William Fox appealed the case to the General Court of the colony and there is no record of its final determination.

[72] Ibid., 51.

[73] *Lancaster County, Will and Deed Book 13, 1736-1743*, 21-22; *Lancaster County Will Book 16, 1758-1763*, 148-149.

dishes, cooking utensils, tools, building materials, candles, and strong beverages (brandy and wine were typically inventoried by the gallon).[74] The operation of a store, however primitive, would have given the Bertrands a way to assist new Huguenot emigrants. French newcomers would have valued having a place to buy necessities (sometimes on credit) from a trusted merchant who spoke their native language and understood their culture.

Other Lancaster lawsuits show that Charlotte was engaged in transatlantic business. In September 1704, Charlotte took legal action against Bristol merchant William Lawson for his refusal to honor letters of credit he had issued to a customer of Charlotte's. Lawson most likely issued the letters of credit to a local planter in exchange for his tobacco. These certificates could then be used as a medium of exchange in the cash-poor colony. After receiving the certificates in exchange for goods, Charlotte submitted them to Lawson or his Virginia agent who refused to honor them. After reviewing the case, the Lancaster justices ordered Lawson's representative to make good on the letters of credit. In this and other cases like it, the Lancaster County Court was functioning as an arbiter of transatlantic

---

[74] Parke Rouse, *James Blair of Virginia* (Chapel Hill, NC, 1971), 176.

business.[75] The fact that Charlotte was doing business with a variety of merchants based in England between 1701 and 1705 is also significant. In addition to William Lawson, Charlotte was dealing with Bristol merchant Thomas Cooper, Liverpool merchant Thomas Hinde, and two merchants whose British port cities are not specified in the records—William Fletcher and Thomas Mackey.[76] The list of merchants doing business with Charlotte was undoubtedly much longer since the county records only contain the names of those with whom she was in litigation.

As Charlotte struggled to establish her mercantile business in the wake of her husband's death, she formed a partnership with a merchant named Henry Salkeld about 1704. Salkeld was a member of a prominent family of the Cumbria region of northeast England.[77] He was active in trading activities in Virginia and Maryland, with Lancaster's Whitechapel Parish

---

[75] *Lancaster Order Book 5, 1702-1713*, 102 and 113.

[76] For Thomas Cooper, see *Lancaster County Deed Book 9, 1701-1706*, 25. For Thomas Hinde, see Ibid., 45. For Thomas Mackey, see Sparacio, *Lancaster County Deed Book, 1701-1706*, 45-46. For William Lawson, see Ibid., 66. For William Fletcher, see *Lancaster County Order Book 5, 1702-1713*, 18.

[77] Joseph Nicolson and Richard Burn, *The History and Antiquities of the Counties of Westmoreland and Cumberland* (London, 1777), vol. 2, 151-152.

as his base of operations. In August 1706, Salkeld issued a power of attorney to one of Charlotte's neighbors and apparently left on a trip from which he did not return.[78] Six months later, Salkeld's widow issued a document from England that placed the entire American estate of the now deceased merchant in Charlotte's hands. With Salkeld's widow signing her name "Mary Ann Salkeld," and Lancaster tithable tax records suggesting enslaved workers were passed back and forth between Charlotte and the English merchant,[79] it is possible this business partnership was sealed by a marriage linking the families. By the standards of Charlotte's seventeenth-century Huguenot mercantilist culture, sealing such a partnership through marriage made perfect sense. Mary Ann Bertrand turned sixteen in 1706—old enough for marriage by contemporary Virginia standards.

The 1706 power of attorney issued by Mary Ann Salkeld identified Charlotte Bertrand as a widow living on Deep Creek in Lancaster County, Virginia—confirming that she and John had

---

[78] Ruth and Sam Sparacio, *Lancaster County Deed Book, 1701-1706* (McLean, VA, 1995), 98.

[79] Lancaster County Individual Tithables, 1653-1720, B, vol. II, L4 and S, vol. XI, L13, Mary Ball Washington Library, Lancaster, Virginia; *Lancaster County Order Book 5, 1702-1713*, 179, 204, and 232.

reoriented the plantation to the Deep Creek side of the property and that their business plan was starting to bear fruit.[80] Records suggest that by this time the Bertrand plantation was becoming known as *Deep Creek* as the Bertrand family was putting its stamp on the plantation that would eventually be known as *Belle Isle*.[81]

Through the intercolonial and transatlantic ships that called regularly at the *Deep Creek* landing, Charlotte had a convenient mail system to communicate with family and friends in English America and in Europe. As her husband's 1701 will demonstrated, the Virginia Bertrands knew the circumstances in which John's nephew, Paul Bertrand III, was growing up in London. When Paul Bertrand, Jr.—a Huguenot-Anglican minister in Maryland—died there about 1690, his widow, Marie Gribelin, returned to London. Upon her return, she leaned heavily on her family for support—especially her brother Simon who was a noted Huguenot engraver in the Savoy district where Charlotte lived during her time in London. Charlotte almost certainly knew that Gribelin produced engravings to illustrate the first attempt at a comprehensive history of Virginia. Robert

---

[80] Sparacio, *Lancaster County Deed Book, 1706-1710*, 13.

[81] *Lancaster County Will Book 16*, 105-106.

Beverley's *The History and Present State of Virginia* was published in 1704, seventeen years before Charlotte's death.[82] A French edition of this work was printed in Amsterdam in 1707.

Charlotte's skillful and determined management of the *Deep Creek* plantation and its trading operations succeeded in putting it on a sound financial footing—enabling her children to become influential members of the Lancaster gentry. In 1685, Charlotte left France for England with a noble pedigree and few resources to back it up.[83] In 1687, she sailed to Virginia with her new husband determined that the children she hoped to bear in the new world would grow up in the Protestant faith as she had and eventually enjoy the material advantages she had left behind when she escaped from France. After thirty-four years of struggle in Virginia, Charlotte's American dream came to fruition.

---

[82] Robert Beverley, *The History and Present State of Virginia, ed., Louis B. Wright* (Chapel Hill, 1947).

[83] That Charlotte Jolly Bertrand fled to England with little money is confirmed by her receipt of a charitable grant in 1686; Royal Bounty, Ms 1, folio 88 (Joly), Huguenot Library, University College, London.

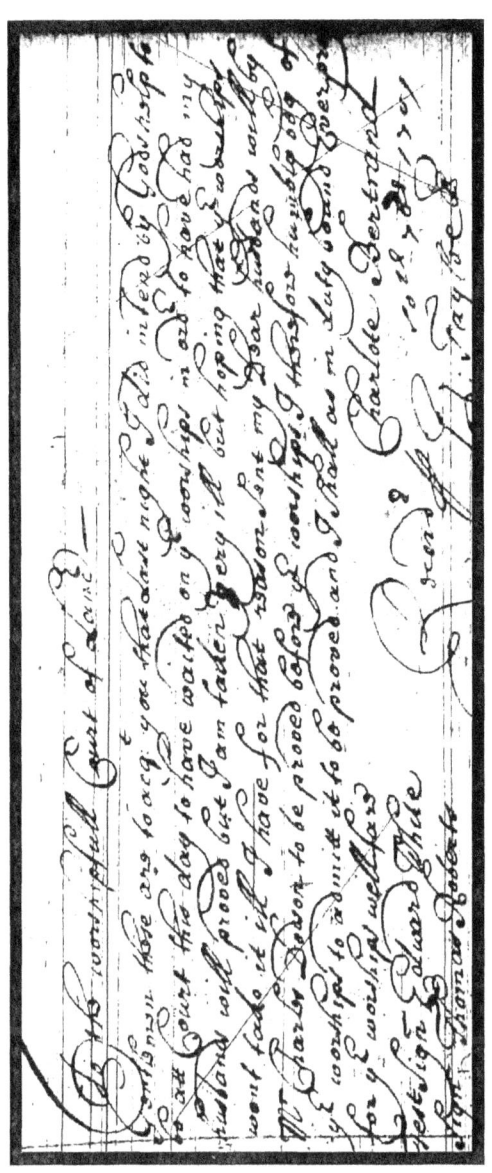

Charlotte Bertrand's Codicil to John Bertrand's 1701 Will
Courtesy, Library of Virginia, Richmond

6
The Mercantile Partnership of William and Mary Ann Bertrand, 1713-1761

The provisions of John Bertrand's will stipulated that his son William (c.1688-1761) would inherit the Bertrand plantation upon reaching the age of twenty-one. But the county records show that William's mother continued her management activities at least until 1713—the year William turned twenty-five. During her twelve years or more of running *Deep Creek* and its trading operations, Charlotte Bertrand forged a business partnership through which her son and daughter, Mary Ann (1690-1750), effectively shared the plantation. While this was a highly unusual arrangement in the patriarchal legal and social context of colonial Virginia, it was a very common practice among seventeenth-century merchant families in western France.

The notion that Henry Salkeld was a son-in-law as well as business partner of Charlotte Bertrand is credible because his interactions with Charlotte fit the pattern of her later relationship with her well-documented son-in-law Charles Ewell (c.1682–

1722). Charles came from a family that was part of the Presbyterian Puritan community on the Eastern Shore of Virginia, with close ties to the Presbyterian minister/merchant Francis Makemie.[84] Charles' father, James Ewell (1641-1704), was an English emigrant from Kent who arrived in Accomac County about 1666.[85] After growing up in Accomac County, Charles began purchasing land there in 1706. Later that year, he was acquiring land in Lancaster County, too. In 1710, he sold the

---

[84] Charles Ewell's brother, Mark, was married to Comfort Hope, cousin of Francis Makemie's wife, Noami Anderson. Comfort Hope's mother, Temperance Waddelow, was the sister of Noami's father, William Anderson; *Accomac County Wills, 1692-1715*, 209. The second husband of Naomi Anderson Makemie's sister, Comfort, was Charles Ewell's brother, Solomon; Nora Miller Turman and Gladys Lee Hamilton, "The Daughter of Francis Makemie," *The Colonial Genealogist, 13.*

[85] James Ewell's identification with Kent is documented in the 1725 will of Edward Ewell of Kent naming "the heirs of James Ewell, late of Accomac Creek in Accomac County on the Eastern Shore of Virginia;" PRC 17/84/24, Canterbury Cathedral Archives. The Edward Ewell who wrote this will was the brother of James and not his father as Ewell family historians have often assumed. For James Ewell's year of birth, see *Accomac County Order Book, 1676-1678*, 10. For his will filed June 7, 1704, see *Accomac County Wills (1692-1715)*, 347. For James' arrival in Virginia about 1666, see *Accomac County Order Book, 1667-1670*, 77.

last of his Accomac County land to complete his transition to Lancaster.[86] Charles married Mary Ann Bertrand about 1710 and took up residence at the *Deep Creek* plantation. Whitechapel tithable tax lists for 1710 and 1711 suggest that enslaved workers were being transferred to Charles as Mary Ann's dowery and the Bertrands had a new business partner.[87]

Charles Ewell's capacity to invest in the development of the *Deep Creek* transit and trading operations is clear. His family's close connection to the Anderson/Makemie family—wealthy merchants on the Eastern Shore—gave the Bertrands a promising new trading relationship. Like his father, Charles was a builder in a colony where builders were in demand. Some of the records describe him as a bricklayer—meaning he constructed buildings using brick. He apparently was successful in this profession at a very young age because he arrived in Lancaster County as a twenty-four-year-old flush with cash. Between 1706 and 1708 he paid 235 pounds sterling in cash for 650 acres near the harbor of Lancaster's Corrotoman River.

---

[86] JoAnn Riley McKey, *Accomac County, Virginia Court Order Abstracts, 1703-1710* (Berwyn Heights, MD, 2001), vol. 10, 84, 95, and 153; Ibid., 1710-1714, vol. 11, 4.

[87] *Lancaster County Order Book 5, 1702-1713*, 255, 278-279, and 296.

While there is no documentary evidence for the Ewell family legend that Charles built the Virginia statehouse in Williamsburg (completed in 1704), his capacity to pay cash for land in 1706 suggests he participated in a lucrative construction project somewhere in the colony during the time that its signature building was under construction. The fact that he was only twenty-two years old in 1704 further suggests any role he might have played in a project as large as the statehouse would have been as a sub-contractor.[88]

Charles Ewell's construction business and the cash it generated likely made a significant contribution to the *Deep Creek* operations. Charlotte understood that an in-house builder could construct or expand plantation homes, loading docks, and warehouses to improve the *Deep Creek* infrastructure for the family trading business. But she also recognized that gaining Ewell's full participation in these business activities would require making him a resident partner of the *Deep Creek* operations. This presented several challenges. At the time of the marriage, Charles Ewell already owned a very good plantation with a house in another part of the county. William Bertrand was

---

[88] Sparacio, *Lancaster County Deed Book, 1706-1710,* 19-20, 46-47.

twenty-two years old and had just inherited his two-thirds share of the *Deep Creek* plantation (the other third belonging to Charlotte until her death, when William would receive that, too). The plantation was entailed through John Bertrand's will, so neither Charlotte nor William could sell any part of it to Charles Ewell.

But Charlotte wasn't about to let the legal restrictions of the English practice of entailment prevent her plans for the *Deep Creek* business from moving forward. Once again she leaned heavily on her French merchant identity for a solution to her dilemma. On December 8, 1712, Charlotte surrendered 125 acres of her one-third life interest in the 924-acre plantation to her son William.[89] On the following day, December 9, 1712, William granted Charles Ewell a lease on the same 125 acres. Charles paid twenty pounds sterling and two enslaved workers for a lease for two lifetimes—his own and that of his first born child, Mary Ann Ewell. Once again, ownership of enslaved persons was being transferred within the family partnership.[90]

The 125-acre tract leased by Charles Ewell was part of the original 500-acre Thomas Powell patent. It fronted the

---

[89] *Lancaster County Deed Book 9,* 421-422

[90] Ibid., 434-435.

Rappahannock River, extending to the mouth of Deep Creek. It was a well-treed portion of the plantation, with a fine orchard.[91] This tract also included the house where Charlotte lived.

Charles and Mary Ann Ewell clearly placed a high value on this tract. He renewed his lease in 1719,[92] and Mary Ann retained it until her death in 1750.[93] Charlotte had engineered a family business partnership that tied Charles Ewell and her daughter, Mary Ann, to *Deep Creek* and to her son, William Bertrand. Though legally owned by William, the plantation would be effectively shared by Charlotte's two children for the next 38 years. This was an arrangement rooted in Charlotte's Huguenot mercantilist instincts and her adherence to Saintonge egalitarian inheritance customs.

---

[91] A description of the orchard on this property is given in the 1722 will of Charles Ewell; *Lancaster County Will Book 10,* 376-378. For the use of orchards by Virginians during this period, see Rhys Isaac, *The Transformation of Virginia, 1740-1790* (Chapel Hill, NC, 1999), 34.

[92] *Lancaster County Deed Book 11, 1714-1728,* 136. For the renewal of the lease Ewell paid 20 pounds sterling once again, but this time there was no transfer of enslaved workers.

[93] Fairfax Papers, White Chapel Parish Rental Roll for 1750, Box VII, BR Box 233, Huntington Library, San Marino, California.

In 1713, William Bertrand, age twenty-five, married a woman who was part of the Huguenot refugee community of the Rappahannock region. Susannah Foushee (1695-c.1745) was the daughter of Huguenots James and Marie Foushee—John and Charlotte's closest friends. William and Susannah moved into their own home that was most likely located near the site of the existing 1767 *Belle Isle* plantation house.[94]

At Charlotte's death in 1721, William and Mary Ann were operating the *Deep Creek* trading businesses. Mary Ann's management of the Bertrand store is documented in April 1722.[95] William Bertrand was apparently responsible for the tobacco storage and trading part of the business. He was sworn in as a Tobacco Receiver by the Lancaster County justices in October 1722. In this capacity, William was responsible for weighing and inspecting tobacco for the growers who deposited their crop with him. He certified the quality of the tobacco and provided secure

---

[94] Mary Ann Bertrand and Charles Ewell had five children: Mary Ann (c.1710--c. 1750), Charles (c.1712—1747), Charlotte (c.1714—c.1782), Bertrand (c. 1716—1794), and Solomon (c.1718—1767). William Bertrand and Susannah Foushee had one surviving child: Mary Ann (1717-1770); George Harrison Sanford King, Msslk5823a, Virginia Historical Society Library, Richmond.

[95] *Lancaster County, Virginia Will Book 10, 1709-1727*, 392-397.

storage. He then issued tobacco notes to the grower who could use them as legal tender within the county.

William Bertrand's work as a Tobacco Receiver suggests the Lancaster County Court had by this time designated his *Deep Creek* wharf a public landing and storage area for tobacco, grain, and other merchandise. The Virginia Assembly periodically enacted statutes regulating this business. William Bertrand was required to accept and safely store crops and merchandise for citizens of the county at the fees established by the Assembly. Because William made the all-important decisions about the quality of the tobacco he received, he had by 1722 become a man of considerable influence in Lancaster County.[96]

Records show that William was being assisted in this work by at least two other members of the Bertrand family, including Mary Ann's next husband.[97] Charles Ewell died in 1722 leaving Mary Ann a wealthy widow with five young children. She married William Ballandine (d. 1736) in December

---

[96] *Lancaster Order Book 7, 1721-1729*, 65. For the influential role played by tobacco receivers and inspectors, see Isaac, *The Transformation of Virginia*, 30 and 93.

[97] Ruth and Sam Sparacio, *Lancaster County Order Book, 1729-1743* (McLean, VA, 1998), 8.

1724.[98] Ballandine was a ship captain who had transported tobacco from the Rappahannock region to Liverpool.[99] As a member of the Bertrand family partnership, he operated his own 40-foot sloop to bring tobacco and grain to the Deep Creek warehouse from planters upriver. He could also make trading expeditions to the Caribbean islands or other ports beyond the Chesapeake Bay.[100]

By the end of 1724, Willian Bertrand could also call on the assistance of his father-in-law, James Foushee. After the death of his wife in October 1724,[101] Foushee left his Richmond County plantation to his son and moved to the *Deep Creek* plantation where he remarried and leased a tract of land from his

---

[98] Lancaster County Register of Marriages, 16 December, 1724. Mary Ann Bertrand Ewell and William Ballandine had two daughters: Frances (c. 1728-1792) and Hannah (c.1730-1770). Ballandine brought with him two sons from a previous marriage: William and John.

[99] Edmund Berkeley, Jr., ed., *The Diary, Correspondence, and Papers of Robert "King" Carter of Virginia, 1701-1732*, Robert Carter to John Pemberton, January 28, 1723/24, http//www.christchurch1735.org. Ibid., ff24v.

[100] *Lancaster Will and Deed Book 13, 1736-1743*, 15, 21-22.

[101] George Harrison Sanford King, ed., *The Registers of North Farnham Parish, 1663-1814 and Lunenburg Parish, 1783-1800, Richmond County, Virginia* (Fredericksburg, VA, 1966), 64.

son-in-law for the last five years of his life. James Foushee brought his own contingent of enslaved workers to produce tobacco and wheat on his Deep Creek lease.[102] Both Foushee and Ballandine were issuing tobacco notes to growers who were using the Bertrand landing and storage facilities.

The *Deep Creek* tobacco trading operations were seriously disrupted in March 1732. Tougher government standards for the inspection of tobacco generated a high degree of hostility among smaller growers who could not afford to have their lower quality tobacco discarded. Angry mobs protested the new inspection regime by storming the tobacco warehouses at Deep Creek and burning them to the ground. Much of the tobacco stored in the warehouses was consumed in the fire. The report submitted to the Lancaster justices on the conflagration

---

[102] *Lancaster County Deed and Will Book 12*, 1726-1736, 144, 157-159. Foushee's will assigned four enslaved persons to his wife Ruth (Tom, Biley, Fillis, and the girl Fillis), two to his son John (young Tom and Sonny), three to his daughter Charlotte Tebbs (Abraham, young Jack, and Rebecah), and three to his daughter Susannah Bertrand (Charles, Dick, and Hector). James Foushee's grandson, William Foushee (son of John), became mayor of the city of Richmond in 1782; *The Huguenot* (Founders of Manakin), no. 11 (1941-1943), 89-94.

named William Ballandine as one of those who lost tobacco in the fire.[103]

The 1732 riot was to have long term consequences for the Bertrand tobacco trading business. The warehouses on Deep Creek were rebuilt, but by April 1738, William Bertrand was no longer operating a public landing for the county. William was apparently renting his tobacco facilities and a small parcel of land to Lancaster County which was by then leasing the landing and warehouses on Deep Creek to Bertrand's neighbor, William Sydnor. Though he was no longer the proprietor of any of the Deep Creek warehouses, William continued to benefit from this business through the rental income he received and the ease with which he could participate in the tobacco trade generated there.[104]

By 1720, Virginia's indentured servants had largely been replaced by enslaved workers imported from Africa or the Caribbean. Records show the *Deep Creek* work force followed

---

[103] Richard S. Hutchinson, *Lancaster County, Virginia Abstracts of Order Book 8, Part One, 1728-1737* (Millsboro, DE, 2014), 56.

[104] Richard S. Hutchinson, *Lancaster County, Virginia Abstracts of Wills, Administrations, Deeds, Inventories, Etc., 1726-1735* (Berwyn Heights, MD, 2011), 33.

this trend. The 1722 estate inventory of Charles Ewell, lists twenty-one enslaved persons and one indentured servant at *Deep Creek*.[105] A tragic incident at the end of 1725 offers a revealing window into the lives of these enslaved residents of the Bertrand plantation. An enslaved man named George, who belonged to Mary Ann Bertrand's husband, William Ballandine,[106] was brought before the Lancaster County court on January 15, 1726, and arraigned for the murder of an enslaved man named Harry. The victim belonged to William Bertrand. George, who had been trained as a bricklayer by Charles Ewell, entered a plea of "not guilty." When the court met on January 27, the justices questioned five enslaved persons and two other witnesses. The diverse group of witnesses called suggests the incident took

---

[105] The enslaved African Virginians listed at *Deep Creek* in the 1722 will of Charles Ewell were Ben, Betty, Betty, Bristow, Bristow, Comfort, Fortune, George, Jenny, Joe, Joe, Judy, Letty, Nanny, Robin, Sarah, Sarry, Sue, Sukey, Toney, and Young Betty. The indentured servant was Margaret Malone; *Lancaster County Will Book 10*, 376-378.

[106] William Ballandine's 1736 will lists fifteen enslaved African Virginians then living at Deep Creek—Davie, Jimmy, Robert, Fill, Molly, Cate, Jenny, Robin, Bristol, Fortune, Jack, Bricker, Pompey, Duke, and Sue—and one indentured servant, Charles Murphy; *Lancaster Will and Deed Book 13, 1736-1743*, 15, 21-22.

place in a relatively public setting—possibly the Bertrand landing or store.

After weighing the testimony, the court ruled that George was guilty of manslaughter. The justices then sentenced George to be "forewith burnt in his hand at the barr." The sheriff immediately carried out the sentence. Once George had been publicly branded, the court adjourned.[107] One historian has noted that it was customary for an enslaved man who was being publicly punished in this way to shout "God Save the King!" as the hot iron was brought out, to celebrate having escaped capital punishment.[108] The repetition of names in the Deep Creek inventories of the enslaved between 1722 and 1778 suggests the plantation's African Virginian community was a stable and well established part of *Belle Isle*. This enslaved labor force clearly provided useful skills and a depth of knowledge that was essential to the agricultural and business operations generating wealth for the Bertrands.

The successful business partnership of John and Charlotte Bertrand's children, William and Mary Ann, continued

---

[107] *Lancaster County Order Book 7, 1721-1729*, 192-194.

[108] Isaac, *The Transformation of Virginia, 1740-1790*, 92.

after the death of Willian Ballandine in 1736,[109] and placed them in a secure position as respected members of the Lancaster gentry. This was confirmed by Mary Ann's third documented marriage in 1742 to the wealthy Lancaster court justice and merchant James Ball (cousin of George Washington's mother, Mary Ball Washington). This Bertrand/Ball family alliance was strengthened by the marriages of two of Mary Ann's sons to daughters of James Ball and the marriage of one of Mary Ann's daughters to the grandson of James Ball's brother. From her home, Mary Ann had a clear view of *Bewdley*, James Ball's home that can still be seen directly across Deep Creek from the Belle Isle State Park visitor center.[110]

At her death in 1750, Mary Ann still held the lease for the *Deep Creek* home her mother gave her. By that time the land

---

[109] *Lancaster County Will Book 13, 1736-1743*, 15.

[110] Charles Ewell, Jr. (c.1712–1747) married Sarah Ball (1712—c.1756), Solomon Ewell (c.1718–1768) married Eve Ball Taylor (1713–1778), and Hannah Ballandine (c.1730—c.1770) married William Montague (1730–1784) —grandson of William Ball.

that went with the home had increased from 125 to 225 acres.[111] Mary Ann's husband Charles Ewell had built a large two-story addition onto the home with walls and/or chimneys constructed with bricks that he made. Enslaved bricklayers like George performed this work.[112] Bringing together the results of the 2006 study of *Belle Isle* sites by the William and Mary Center for Archeological Research with various records already cited makes it possible to pinpoint the location of this large home. The Bertrand/Ewell home was situated between the present-day state park visitor center and the point where Deep Creek flows into the Rappahannock.

The archeological study identified early eighteenth-century brick pier/footing features for a large building that was in use until about 1750. The excavation at this site revealed a large quantity of hand-made brick and the oyster shell material typically used for interior wall plaster in eighteenth-century

---

[111] Fairfax Papers, White Chapel Parish Rental Roll for 1750, Box VII, BR Box 233, Huntington Library, San Marino, California. The 1750 will of Mary Ann Bertrand Ball lists two enslaved African Virginians—Jenny and Hannah; *Lancaster Deed and Will Book 14, 1743-1750*, 285-286.

[112] *Lancaster County Will Book 10*, 376-378. For Charles Ewell's work in making bricks, see *Lancaster County, Virginia Deed Book 11, 1714-1728*, 252.

Chesapeake buildings. There were also some fragments of window pane glass. Artifacts recovered from the site include fragments of ceramic tableware, ceramic cooking and storage containers, glass containers, white clay pipe stems, gun flint spalls, glass jewelry beads, and a child's porcelain doll.[113] Archeological evidence suggests this large home was destroyed by fire in the middle of the eighteenth century and was never rebuilt.

The working partnership between Mary Ann and William apparently loosened with her 1742 marriage to James Ball. Some of the enslaved workers held by Mary Ann's deceased husbands were moving into the ownership of her brother as most of Mary Ann's children were moving to Prince William County.[114] Six of her nine children and stepchildren

---

[113] William and Mary Center for Archeological Research, *Archeological Evaluation of Sites 44LA147 and 44LA175, Belle Isle State Park, Lancaster County Virginia*, 53. The Bertrand/Ewell home stood at site 44LA147.

[114] *Prince William County Deed Book D*, 338-341; John Frederick Dorman, *Prince William County, Virginia Will Book C, 1733-1744* (Washington DC, 1956), 97-99.

made this move.[115] Following the example of their parents and grandparents, these Bertrand descendants formed a business partnership—opening a store and a tobacco trading and warehousing business at the port of Dumfries on the Potomac River.[116] When this Prince William partnership purchased an iron works on the Occoquan River and subsequently went bankrupt,[117] William Bertrand took decisive action to protect his *Deep Creek* plantation and its related businesses from the creditors of his sister's children. The creditors, who were pursuing William's nephews and nieces, would have been

---

[115] Mary Ann's children moving to Prince William County were Charles Ewell Jr. (wife Sarah Ball), Charlotte Ewell Gallahue (husband Darby), Bertrand Ewell (wife Frances Kenner), and Frances Ballandine (never married). Her stepchildren going to Prince William were William Ballandine, Jr. and John Ballandine. Mary Ann's children remaining in Lancaster County were Mary Ann Ewell White (husband Isaac), Solomon Ewell (wife Eve Ball Taylor), and Hannah Ballandine Montague (husband William).

[116] William Waller Hening and Samuel Shepherd, ed., *The Statutes at Large of Virginia from October 1792 to December 1806* (Richmond, VA, 1835-36), vol. 1, 264; John Frederick Dorman, *Virginia Revolutionary Pension Applications* (Washington DC, 1958), vol. 35, 31-36.

[117] Ruth and Sam Sparacio, *Deed Abstracts of Prince William County, 1749-1752/1761-1764* (McLean, VA, 1989), 32, 107-111, 120-121, 133-135, 138-140, 1763-1768, 67-70, 75-77, 87-88, 106-107, and 111-112.

looking for any interest these Bertrand family members might have in the *Deep Creek* store, public landing, and tobacco/grain warehouses in Lancaster County. Did the creditors know that the 1719 Charles Ewell *Deep Creek* lease (by then encompassing 225 acres of the plantation) included the lifetime of Bertrand Ewell—one of the bankrupt partners in Prince William County?

William Bertrand knew this and understood all too well the threat the Occoquan bankruptcy presented to the Deep Creek plantation. William responded to the crisis by putting in place a creative legal strategy. His 1759 will named Thomas Bertrand Griffin (1735-1778)—the oldest son of his daughter—as his heir.[118] On July 18, 1760, William executed a tripartite deed with his heir and one of the wealthiest men in the county—Charles Carter (1732-1806). Carter was a grandson of Robert "King" Carter, and was then managing the Carter operations at Corrotoman in Lancaster County. Later he would move to his

---

[118] William Bertrand's daughter, Mary Ann (c. 1717-1770), married Leroy Griffin (1711-1750) of Richmond County in 1734. Their other children were Elizabeth (b. 1737), Leroy, Jr. (1738-1775), Corbin (1741-1813), William (b. 1743), Samuel (1746-1810), Cyrus (1748-1810), and John Tayloe (b. 1750); King, MssIk5823a, Virginia Historical Society Library, Richmond; *The Virginia Magazine of History and Biography*, 1, no. 3, (Jan. 1894), 255-256.

plantation on the James River where his daughter would marry "Light Horse Harry" Lee.[119] By this agreement, William insulated the plantation from potential creditors by handing over his entire estate to Carter in trust for his twenty-five-year-old grandson and heir. William was to have free use of his estate until his death.[120] William Bertrand died in the spring of 1761. When the storm passed and the creditors faded away, Charles Carter delivered an unencumbered inheritance to Thomas Bertrand Griffin.

The inventory of William Bertrand's estate reveals that he lived in a house of six rooms, of which the two principal rooms were the hall and chamber on the first floor.[121] The inventory also makes reference to an older and smaller house nearby.[122] Other buildings listed include the stand-alone kitchen, cellar, dairy, and store. With the addition of slave quarters and

---

[119] Albert H. Tillson and the *Dictionary of Virginia Biography*, "Charles Carter (1732-1806)," *Encyclopedia Virginia*, Virginia Humanities, April 19, 2017; Clifford Dowdey, *The Virginia Dynasties: The Emergence of "King" Carter and the Golden Age* (Boston, 1969), 364.

[120] *Lancaster County Will Book 16*, 105-106.

[121] Camille Wells, "Belle Isle."

[122] *Lancaster County Will Book 16, 1758-1763*, 148-149.

unnamed storage buildings, the Bertrand plantation would have had the appearance of a small village in 1761.

William Bertrand's will shows that the transition from indentured servants to enslaved laborers at his plantation was complete. There were twenty-eight enslaved African Virginians and no indentured servants living at *Deep Creek* at the time of his death.[123] William's half-century ownership was by far the longest tenure of any of the plantation's colonial patent holders.

---

[123] Ibid. William Bertrand's estate inventory lists the following enslaved African Virginians at *Deep Creek* in 1761: Will, More, Nan, Frank, Billey, Jenny, Daniel, Betty, Criss, Winney, Jack, Richmond, Grasnier, Sampson, Charles, Fortune, Sarah, Tom, Cato, Dan, Doming, Sarah, Suzis, Rose, Tom, Jenny, Betty, and Harry.

**Detail of *A New Map of Virginia, Mary-Land,
and the improved parts of Pennsylvania and New Jersey***
John Senex, 1719
Courtesy, Library of Congress, Geography and Map Division
The map view is roughly centered on the site of Belle Isle Plantation.

7
Thomas Bertrand Griffin and the Belle Isle Plantation House, 1761-1778

Sometime after inheriting the plantation in 1761, Thomas Bertrand Griffin (1735-1778) gave it the name *Belle Isle*. Apparently neither William Bertrand nor his parents bothered to brand the plantation or any of its homes. In his 1760 tripartite deed William referenced two of the names by which the plantation had been known—*Powell's Quarter* and *Deep Creek* — but did not specify his personal preference.[124] William's failure to mention *Belle Isle* in this document suggests this name was not in use in 1760. But when William's grandson inherited the plantation in 1761, the fashion of the Virginia aristocracy called for important colonial seats to have names. It is not surprising that Thomas Bertrand Griffin chose a French name for his plantation. His mother, Mary Ann, was the child of a Huguenot marriage and would have grown up speaking French

---

[124]*Lancaster County Will Book 16*, 105-106.

in her parents' Deep Creek home. Thomas and his siblings were half French by blood and likely had some facility in the language, too.[125]

Five years after inheriting the plantation, Thomas Bertrand Griffin married Judith Burwell (1744-1769) of *Carter's Grove*. She was the daughter of Carter Burwell, a grandson of Robert "King" Carter for whom *Carter's Grove* was named. In 1767, Thomas and Judith began construction of an elegant home that would be more in keeping with the architectural style of their era.[126] It is reasonable to assume that Judith had some influence on the design of a new *Belle Isle* home. Though considerably smaller, this plantation house closely follows the early Georgian Virginia architecture of the mansion her father built at his *Carter's Grove* plantation between 1751 and 1755.

---

[125] The earliest documented use of the name *Belle Isle* for the Bertrand plantation was the obituary article for Thomas Bertrand Griffin; *The Virginia Gazette*: *Dixon and Hunter*, May 8, 1778, 7, Colonial Williamsburg Digital Library.

[126] A dendrochronological study authored by Camille Wells, Edward R. Cook, and William J. Callahan shows that the cutting date for the wood in the center and oldest section of the *Belle Isle* plantation house was 1767; correspondence from Camille Wells to the author March 20, 2014.

Judith was 11 years old when her father's home was completed and she could well have had access to building plans and artisans who participated in its construction.[127]

Visitors arrived at the new *Belle Isle* home by way of a mile-long avenue that ended at the forecourt of a complex consisting of the main house and two dependency buildings symmetrically placed on either side of it. This complex of buildings was oriented to the landward side of the plantation rather than to the river as the home that John and Charlotte passed on to their daughter had been. The elegance of the main house is confirmed by the well-appointed paneling installed in every room extending through both floors in the same way the interior of Carter's Grove was designed. The especially impressive paneling from the first floor and stairwell of the home was purchased by Henry Francis DuPont in 1928 for $25,000. The wealthy industrialist used these architectural features in his

---

[127] For Judith Burwell Griffin's family and the 1755 Carter's Grove mansion, see Daphne Gentry and the *Dictionary of Virginia Biography*, "Carter Burwell (1716-1756)," *Encyclopedia Virginia,* Virginia Humanities, August 21, 2014.

Winterthur mansion in Wilmington, Delaware, where much of it can still be seen.[128]

Thomas Bertrand Griffin's house had a central passage plan—a paneled entry provided access to the parlor and dining room. The presence of a room dedicated to dining was a recent innovation in Virginia homes. The third room on the first floor was the chamber located behind the parlor. From the entry room the stairway to the right led to the second floor with three finely appointed bedrooms. This cube-shaped house was intended to be the first stage of construction with two wings to follow.[129] The couple's plan to expand their home was likely set aside after Judith's untimely death in November 1769. A son and daughter died at birth and were buried in the *Belle Isle* colonial graveyard with her.[130]

Thomas' tribute to his wife in his will indicates that his grief over her death was profound and enduring. He poured his

---

[128] Ron Fuchs in a paper delivered to the Association for the Preservation of Virginia Antiquities on March 18, 2004. Henry du Pont purchased the paneling from antiques dealer Charles MacLellan of Wilmington, Delaware.

[129] Wells, "Belle Isle."

[130] *Virginia Gazette*, Rind, November 30, 1769, 2, Colonial Williamsburg Digital Library.

energies into improvements to the plantation as he purchased adjacent properties. With the tract he purchased from the Newby family he was able to reopen a road from the Bertrand tobacco/grain warehouse to the Ball grain mill that had been closed to William Bertrand in 1749. This road also provided easier access for transporting tobacco from the Morratico plantations to the Bertrand warehouse and landing. Griffin's targeted acquisition of the Newby tract suggests this part of the Bertrand business was still in operation during the early years of his ownership of Belle Isle. Controlling adjacent properties also made it possible for Griffin to construct the mile-long avenue leading to the entrance of his new plantation house.[131]

Thomas Bertrand Griffin also responded to his intense personal loss by investing himself in public service as a church vestryman, Lt. Colonel of the Lancaster militia, and clerk of the Lancaster County court. On July 18, 1776, Lancaster's justices

---

[131] For Thomas Bertrand Griffin's purchase of land from Mary Newby, widow of Henry Newby, see *Lancaster County, Virginia Deed Book 19, 1770-1782*, 172. For the granting of administration of Henry Newby's estate to his widow, Mary, see *Lancaster County Order Book 12, 1764-1767*, 32. For the road leading through this property that William Bertrand wanted to remain open, see *Lancaster County Deed and Will Book 14, 1743-1750*, 238.

held their first court after the Declaration of Independence. The justices and court officers, including Thomas Bertrand Griffin, swore their allegiance to the new commonwealth. By this action they formally renounced their previously sworn allegiance to the British king, George III.[132]

The war for independence also accelerated the decline in Virginia tobacco production that had begun by 1770. In 1776, the tobacco produced in Virginia represented less than 25 percent of what it had been before the war. Many planters were switching to food crops to support the war effort. It is reasonable to assume that the tobacco storage and trading businesses of Thomas Bertrand Griffin at Belle Isle and his Ewell cousins in Dumfries ended their operations during these years.[133] By securing the position as Clerk of the County Court, Thomas Bertrand Griffin

---

[132] Margaret H. Tupper, ed., *Christ Church Parish, Lancaster County, Virginia Vestry Book, 1739-1786* (Irvington, VA, 1990), 69-70; Benjamin J. Hillman, ed., *Executive Journals of the Council of Virginia* (Richmond, VA, 1966), vol. 6, June 20, 1754—May 3, 1775, 405; Jett, *Lancaster County, Virginia*, 113.

[133] Emily Jones Salmon and John Salmon, "Tobacco in Colonial Virginia," *Encyclopedia Virginia*, Virginia Humanities, January 29, 2013.

was able to recoup some of his lost income by collecting fees from registrations and the posting of bonds.[134]

In 1775, Thomas was joined at Belle Isle by his younger brother Cyrus Griffin (1748-1810) and his young family. Cyrus had left Virginia in 1766 to pursue an education in Great Britain. He spent five years as a student at Edinburgh University and then studied four years at the Middle Temple—England's premier law school of the time. Cyrus used much of his inheritance to pay for his education and the expense of his 1771 marriage to Lady Christina Stuart, a member of the English nobility. Cyrus and Lady Christina were married without the knowledge or permission of her father, John Stuart, Earl of Traquair. When the Earl, who was Catholic, first learned that his daughter was smitten with Cyrus, he gave strict orders that she be prevented from seeing the impudent Protestant Virginian again. Traquair was clearly not impressed that Cyrus could claim noble linage for being the great grandson of the daughter of a French Huguenot provincial noble.

---

[134] For the influence and income that Thomas Bertrand Griffin gained through his role as Clerk of the Lancaster County Court, see Isaac, *The Transformation of Virginia*, 88-89.

Cyrus and Lady Christina eloped by using Cyrus' legal education to good advantage. Their marriage was registered in Edinburgh on April 29, 1770. Lady Christina Stuart was entered on the marriage record as Miss Christian Stewart, daughter of the deceased Charles Stewart. Having a deceased father removed the usual requirement for an advance publishing of the "banns," so that the marriage ceremony could be legally performed immediately. If Christina's father had been correctly identified, the required waiting period would have given the Earl more than enough time to cancel the marriage, which could not have gone forward without his consent.[135]

When Cyrus and Lady Christina arrived at Belle Isle in 1775, they were in difficult financial straits. After leaving his wife and daughter with Thomas, Cyrus immediately went back to England to seek a share of his wife's family estate. It is likely that he returned to Virginia with little to show for his effort because he was soon in debt to his brother. In March of 1777, Thomas made a gift to Cyrus of the adjacent 75-acre Newby

---

[135] Henry S. Rorer, "Cyrus Griffin: Virginia's First Federal Judge," *Washington and Lee Law Review* 21, issue 2, article 4 (September 1, 1964), 210- 211.

tract.[136] This gift of a Virginia home for Cyrus in an "annex" of Belle Isle and Cyrus' election to public office by Lancaster County in 1776 confirm Lady Christina's residence at Belle Isle from 1775 and her likely role as a part-time hostess for her widowed brother-in-law. Lady Christina's arrival at *Belle Isle* undoubtedly captured the attention of the Lancaster gentry who rarely had the opportunity to socialize with persons who were so highly placed in the British aristocracy.[137]

Thomas Bertrand Griffin did not marry again after the deaths of Judith and their children. For him there would be no little ones growing up at Belle Isle. But his close relationship with Cyrus' family is confirmed by his generous bequest of 500 pounds currency to his "dear little niece, Mary Griffin, daughter

---

[136] For Thomas Bertrand Griffin's gift of 75 acres of land adjacent to Belle Isle to his brother Cyrus, see *Lancaster County, Virginia Deed Book 19, 1770-1782*, 172.

[137] Rorer, "Cyrus Griffin: Virginia's First Federal Judge," 204. Records show that Cyrus was elected to represent Lancaster County in the Virginia House of Delegates as he was preparing to sail home from England. Lord Germaine granted him permission to sail on April 30, 1776; Original Correspondence—Secretaries of State, Miscellaneous, 1771-1776, Griffin, Cyrus—1776, SR 00559, 2, Library of Virginia, Richmond.

of my brother Cyrus."[138] Little Mary Griffin's presence in Thomas' impressive new home may well have brought him a measure of the joy that he had been denied by the tragic deaths of his own children.

---

[138] *Lancaster County Will Book 20*, folio 120.

Detail of Tobacco Landing
A Map of the Most Inhabited Part of Virginia
Joshua Fry and Peter Jefferson, 1755
Courtesy, Library of Congress, Geography and Map Division

8
Corbin Griffin and the End of Belle Isle's Bertrand Era, 1778-1782

When Thomas Bertrand Griffin died in March or April of 1778, he bequeathed *Belle Isle* to his oldest surviving brother Corbin Griffin (1741-1813). His will directed that his land from adjacent counties be equally divided among his other four brothers. All of Thomas' brothers owed money to him at the time of his death (including the already deceased Leroy Griffin). Thomas forgave these debts in his will. The will also directed that the five surviving brothers share equally in his personal estate. The Thomas Bertrand Griffin estate inventory, including thirty-nine enslaved men, women, and children, was valued at more than 5,767 pounds.[139] Neither *Belle Isle* nor the other plantations

---

[139] *Lancaster County Will Book 20*, folio 120. The enslaved African Virginians listed in Thomas Bertrand Griffin's 1778 will were David, Nan, Jenny, Rose and her child Elijah, Winny and her child John, Beth and her child Ellin, Sally and her child Milly, Rachel, Betty, Sam, Billy, Dick, Jacob, Rawleigh, Doming, Criss, Liddy, Nanny, Patt, Phillis, Molly, John, Anthony, Adam, Nan, Frank, Will, Charles, Charles, Planter, Tom, Will, Harry, Dan, and Sam.

Thomas owned were included in this accounting of his net worth.

Corbin Griffin was the first Bertrand descendant to inherit the plantation knowing that he could sell it. In his will, John Bertrand entailed the plantation to legally tie it to his family. Entailment was a limited form of ownership enshrined in British law by which those who inherited had full use of their property but could not mortgage or sell it. The owner could only designate the next heir within the family. In October 1776, three months after independence was declared, the Virginia Assembly met to revise its laws to reflect its new status as a commonwealth. One of the first laws to be changed ended the practice of entailing landed estates. The removal of the legal basis for entailing land represented the end of an era. After 126 years as a British colonial plantation, *Belle Isle* was suddenly part of the commonwealth of Virginia—a newly constituted republic. After seventy-five years of mandatory Bertrand family ownership, *Belle Isle* could legally be sold.[140]

Soon after inheriting *Belle Isle*, Corbin Griffin decided to exercise his recently established legal right to sell it. Corbin

---

[140] Hening, *Statutes at Large*, vol. 9, 226-227.

had a medical practice in York County by 1773. That was the year he purchased a house and adjacent building for his work as a physician in Yorktown.[141] When *Belle Isle* came into his possession, Corbin's mind was on other things. He was deeply involved in the revolutionary struggle against the British. In March 1776, he was helping to provision revolutionary troops at Yorktown. In August 1776, he was selected to be a delegate to the Continental Congress from York County.[142] By the end of 1776, he was serving as surgeon on a Virginia military galley called the *Manley*. When the ship was decommissioned in 1779, he continued to serve the revolutionary cause as surgeon in the naval hospital near Yorktown until the end of the war.[143]

Corbin did not wait for the war to end to put his Lancaster County plantation on the market. On July 10, 1778, he placed the following advertisement in the *Virginia Gazette*:

---

[141] *Colonial Yorktown's Main Street: Historic Resource Study,* nps.gov.

[142] *Virginia Gazette,* Purdie, August 30, 1776, 3, Colonial Williamsburg Digital Library.

[143] Bounty Records, Pension Application of Corbin Griffin (R-56), Correspondence between John H. Smith and Virginia Governor John B. Floyd on August 22, 1850 and September 14, 1850, Library of Virginia, Richmond.

> For Sale, a valuable plantation on the banks of the Rappahannock, in Lancaster County, twelve miles above Urbanna, conveniently situated between two creeks, and abounding with fish, oysters, and wildfowl. It contains about 100 acres of marsh, which at a small expense may be converted into valuable meadows, the soil equal almost to any in Virginia, for tobacco, grain, cotton, and flax; and it has, for the accommodation of a family, an elegant new brick house, with all other necessary buildings. A choice of cattle, sheep, and hogs may be had with the above land.[144]

Plantations were not selling while the war for independence raged. Potential buyers would have had a difficult time negotiating with Corbin Griffin in September 1781, because he was incarcerated on a British prison ship under the command of Lord Cornwallis. Corbin was arrested by British troops as he tried to load his family and household furniture into a boat to evacuate them from British occupied Yorktown. His wife, Mary Berkeley, managed to send a message to the American

---

[144] *Virginia Gazette*, July 10, 1778, Colonial Williamsburg Digital Library.

commander, General Nelson, who negotiated with Cornwallis for Corbin's release.[145]

Corbin Griffin was not the only member of the family who was "all in" for the revolutionary cause. Five of his brothers were participating in the war effort as well. Leroy Griffin was appointed Major to the battalion of Minute-men in the lower district of the Northern Neck before his death in November of 1775. Thomas Bertand Griffin served in the Lancaster militia as Lt. Colonel and when the Virginia Gazette reported his death in 1778, it described him as a "warm patriot." Samuel Griffin was a colonel and deputy adjutant general in the Continental Line and a member of the State Board of War in 1781. William Griffin was a colonel commanding Virginia militia in 1781.[146]

Cyrus Griffin was a member of the war-time Congress and was providing supplies to the Lancaster County Militia in

---

[145] William P. Palmer, ed., *Calendar of Virginia State Papers and Other Manuscripts, 1652-1781* (Richmond, VA, 1875), vol. 7, 490; Dorman, *Virginia Revolutionary Pension Applications*, vol. 47, 67-71.

[146] *The Virginia Magazine of History and Biography* 1, no. 3 (Jan., 1894), 254-256; Virginia Gazette, Purdie, November 10, 1775, 2 and August 9, 1776, 2, Colonial Williamsburg Digital Library; Jett, *Lancaster County, Virginia,* 388; Virginia Board of War, Samuel Griffin . . . # 44393, Library of Virginia, Richmond.

April 1778. But just before the war broke out, Cyrus was engaged in a diplomatic effort to avert hostilities. On his trip to London to seek a portion of his wife's inheritance in the fall of 1775, he carried a message to Lord Dartmouth (William Legge), the British Secretary of State for the Colonies. Dartmouth had earlier written to Benjamin Franklin and other leaders in America looking for a way to reconcile the differences between Great Britain and the colonies. Cyrus was apparently delivering an American response. But when he arrived at Dartmouth's home on December 30, 1775, it was too late. Dartmouth had given up on finding a peaceful solution and had resigned his position in the government the previous month. He took Griffin's "Plan of Reconciliation," endorsed it, and filed it away. It is not known who was promoting the plan from the American side or whether Lord Dartmouth discussed it with his step-brother, the British Prime Minister, before placing it in his files.[147]

---

[147] *The Virginia Magazine of History and Biography* 8, no. 3 (Jan. 1901), 308; *Biographical Directory of the United States Congress, 1774 to Present,* Griffin, Cyrus (1748-1810). For Cyrus Griffin's presentation of a "Plan for Reconciliation" to Lord Dartmouth in December of 1775, see *The Virginia Magazine of History and Biography* 19, no. 4 (Oct. 1911), 417 and Rorer, "*Cyrus Griffin: Virginia's First Federal Judge,"* 202-203.

Other great-grandchildren of John and Charlotte Bertrand were active in the revolutionary cause. Charles Ewell, Jr.'s sons, Jesse and James, were part of a freeholders' action in Prince William County to sustain Congressional opposition to the Stamp Act in 1775. Jesse was also a member of the Prince William Committee of Safety that was preparing for hostilities with the British in 1775. In addition, Jesse was elected to represent Fairfax County in the Virginia House of Delegates in 1777. Throughout the war, Jesse commanded the county militia while his brother James served as a major. In the fall of 1781, Jesse was ordered to march his regiment in the direction of Philadelphia to mask Washington's advance on Yorktown. Before reaching his goal, Jesse received word that the Battle of Yorktown had ended and he led his troops back home to celebrate the victory.[148]

[148] *Virginia Gazette*, Pinkney, January 12, 1775, 3, Colonial Williamsburg Digital Library; Ibid. Purdie, May 9, 1777, 2; Horace Edwin Hayden, *A Genealogoy of the Glassell Family of Scotland and Virginia* (Wilkes-Barre, PA, 1891), 338-340; Joan W. Peters, *Prince William County, Virginia Patriots and Pensioners* (Westminster, MD, 2010), *1752-1856*, 76, 94, 84, and 157; Paul D. Casdorph, *Confederate General R. S. Ewell: Robert E. Lee's Hesitant Commander* (Lexington, KY, 2014), 3-5; Manassas Journal Messenger, Centennial Edition, 1969, Prince William County, RELIC Digital Library.

Charles Ewell Jr.'s daughter, Marianne, married a physician named James Craik (1730-1814) in 1760. Craik had served as a surgeon with Washington's troops during the French and Indian War in 1756. During the Revolutionary War he was the Continental Army's chief surgeon and after the war he continued to be the close friend and personal physician of George Washington.[149] Bertrand Ewell, who led the Prince William County militia that provided support to Washington's forces after Edward Braddock's defeat in the French and Indian War in 1756, had two sons who are known to have fought in the Revolution. Thomas was a captain in the First Virginia Regiment from 1776 to 1782. Bertrand's younger son, Charles, also served as captain in the First Virginia Regiment and was by 1781 an aid

---

[149] Hayden, *A Genealogy of the Glassell Family*, 341; "From George Washington to James Craik, 8 September 1789," *The Papers of George Washington, Presidential Series*, vol. 4, 8 September 1789—15 January 1790, ed. Dorothy Twoig, 1-2 (Charlottesville, VA, 1993).

to General Lafayette—suggesting that this Bertrand great grandson had some facility in French.[150]

Solomon Ewell's son, James, was a captain in the Lancaster militia.[151] Charlotte Ewell Gallahue's sons, Charles and Jeremiah, served in the Virginia Line during the struggle for independence, following the example of their older brother John who was injured in the French and Indian War. Charles Gallahue was commissioned as a Captain in January of 1777. On May 23, 1777, he was killed in a raid by American forces on Sag Harbor, Long Island. In his will, Charles designated 25 pounds currency to his brother Jeremiah, whose battalion was moving through the Carolinas and Georgia. Knowing that his brother could be in some danger, Charles made the bequest contingent on the young

---

[150] Revolutionary War Bounty Warrants, Reels 1-29, Certificate Issued by Daniel Morgan, Library of Virginia, Richmond; Commission, Charles Ewell, 1778 June 1, #44385, Library of Virginia; Cornwallis Papers: America, Correspondence on Exchanges of Prisoners, etc., 1781-1782, 2-3, Library of Virginia; Letter and Testimony of Charles Ewell . . . #44862, Library of Virginia.

[151] For James Ewell's service in the Lancaster County Militia during the Revolutionary War, see Jett, *Lancaster County, Virginia*, 388.

man returning alive. Hannah Ballandine Montague's son, Thomas, was a private in one of the Virginia militia units.[152]

While not a Bertrand descendant, John Ballandine spent most of his growing up years at *Belle Isle* where he was raised by his step-mother Mary Ann Bertrand Ballandine. Between 1776 and 1781 he developed a cannon foundry at Westham, Virginia, that made an important contribution to the Patriot war effort. The foundry was destroyed in January 1781 by a loyalist raiding force led by Benedict Arnold. One witness later reported that the explosion that blew up the foundry sounded "like an earthquake."[153] Records show that at least 14 of John and Charlotte's 18 great grandsons known to be living in 1775 were directly involved in the struggle for independence.

---

[152] *Magazine of Virginia Genealogy* 49, no. 1, (February 2011), 49-50; Revolutionary War Bounty Warrants, Reels 1-29, Library of Virginia, Richmond; William Armstrong Cozier, ed., *Virginia County Records, vol. II, Virginia County Militia, 1651-1776*, 114, 117, and 119; United States Senate, *The Pension Roll of 1835* (Baltimore, 1992), vol. 3, 514.

[153] Fairfax Harrison, *Landmarks of Old Prince William* (Baltimore, 1987), 436; Isaac Jefferson, "Life of Isaac Jefferson of Petersburg, Virginia, Blacksmith," (1847), 8, *Encyclopedia Virginia*, Virginia Humanities, May 3, 2013.

With Corbin Griffin clearly not in residence at *Belle Isle* after inheriting the plantation, it may be that Cyrus Griffin was the last of the Bertrand descendants to live there. Cyrus owned adjacent property and needed a place to stay when neither the Virginia House of Delegates nor the Continental Congress was in session. He spent thirty years in public service and was a friend and colleague of Washington, Jefferson, Madison, Franklin, John Marshall, and Patrick Henry.[154] There is, however, reason to question whether his marriage to the daughter of a British Earl helped his career in the newly established American republic. The observation of a French traveler and guest of the Griffins during Cyrus' service in the Congress suggests Lady Christina may not have been the ideal hostess for an American government official. Pierre Brissot de Warville described an evening with the Griffins in these words:

> President Griffin ... is a Virginian of good abilities, of an agreeable figure, affable and polite. I saw at his house at dinner, seven or eight women, all dressed in great hats, plumes, etc. It was with pain that I remarked much of pretension in some of these women ... Two among them had their bosoms very

---

[154] Rorer, "Cyrus Griffin: Virginia's First Federal Judge," 201-211.

naked, I was scandalized at this indecency among republicans ... Little wine was drunk after the women retired.[155]

Cyrus Griffin served two terms in the Continental Congress, 1778-1780 and 1787-1788, and was the last president of that body serving under the Articles of Confederation when George Washington was sworn in as President under a new constitution on April 13, 1789.

Cyrus was unsuccessful in his effort to become Thomas Jefferson's replacement as American Ambassador to France in 1789. Lady Christina had two sisters in Paris at the time and seems to have coveted this appointment for her husband. When Cyrus informed Thomas Jefferson of his wife's family connections in Paris and asked for his help in convincing Washington to appoint him to the post, Jefferson politely replied that he did not have a close enough relationship with the President to make such recommendations.[156] While Washington did not send Cyrus to Paris, he described him as "a man of

---

[155] Ibid., 206-207.

[156] "Letter to Thomas Jefferson from Cyrus Griffin, 11 December, 1789," *The Papers of Thomas Jefferson,* vol. 16, 30 November—4 July 1790, ed. Julian P. Boyd (Princeton. NJ, 1961), 14-15.

amiable character and competent abilities" and appointed him to other positions of responsibility—first as Commissioner to the Creek Indians and later as Judge of the U.S. Court for the District of Virginia. Griffin served in that position until his death in 1810.[157]

In February 1782, Corbin Griffin found a buyer for *Belle Isle*. He sold the plantation he inherited from his brother to Ralph Wormeley IV of *Rosegill* for 5,000 pounds in Virginia currency.[158] Wormeley (1715-1790) was a prominent Virginian from a wealthy Middlesex County family. He acquired *Belle Isle* for Nathaniel Burwell, husband of his daughter Mary. Nathaniel was most likely a cousin of Judith Burwell Griffin and a great-grandson of Robert "King" Carter.[159] The ownership of the

---

[157] United States Congress, *Biographical Directory of the United States Congress*, 1774—present, Griffin, Cyrus, (1748-1810).

[158] *Lancaster County Deed Book 19*, 273-274.

[159] For dates and relationships within the Wormeley family of Rosegill, see the website of the Virginia Historical Society http//www.vahistorical.org. For Ralph Wormeley's relationship with Nathaniel Burwell, see Hayden, *A Genealogy of the Glassell Family*, 231. Nathaniel was a frequently used name in the Burwell family. Judith Burwell Griffin had two uncles with sons named Nathaniel—Robert Burwell and Nathaniel Burwell. For information about this family, see Dowdey, *Virginia Dynasties*.

Burwells, however, was short lived. After the death of his wife, Nathaniel Burwell sold the plantation to Rawleigh Downman in 1786.[160]

Corbin Griffin's 1782 sale of his Rappahannock River plantation brought to an end the ninety-year stewardship of *Belle Isle* by the Bertrand family. The colonial plantation that John Bertrand hoped would forever secure a prominent position for his family in Virginia was gone as his great grandsons directed their energies to another vision—creating a new republic.

---

[160] *Lancaster County Deed Book 21, 1782-1793*, folio 61 (2) and folio 62 (1)

**Paneled Entry and Stairwell of the
1767 *Belle Isle* Plantation House, 1935 Photo**
Courtesy, the Winterthur Library: Winterthur Archives
Wilmington, Delaware

Appendix A:
Belle Isle Plantation Timeline
1650—1782

1650 The first Virginia patent for the *Belle Isle* plantation—then called *Powell's Quarter*—is issued to Thomas Powell for 500 acres.

1664 Following the death of his first wife, Thomas Powell enters into a marriage with Jane Catesby, signing an agreement promising her 200 pounds sterling and one-third of his plantation on the Rappahannock River.

1670 Thomas Powell dies leaving the plantation to Rawleigh, his four year old son by Jane Catesby, with his older son Thomas serving as guardian and overseer.

1671 With the death of Thomas Powell, Jr., guardianship of Rawleigh and control of *Powell's Quarter* is granted to Jane Catesby Powell's new husband, John Kyrby.

1684 Rawleigh Powell, age 18, files a lawsuit against his stepfather, John Kyrby, apparently to gain control of his inheritance.

1687 Rawleigh Powell dies and bequeaths 300 acres of *Powell's Quarter* to his sister Ann Dacres and 200 acres to his step-father John Kyrby.

1690 Ann Dacres sells her 300 acres of *Powell's Quarter* to William Loyd of North Farnham Parish in Richmond County, where John Bertrand is serving as minister.

1691 John Kyrby sells his 200 acres of the plantation to John Loyd, son and heir of the now deceased William Loyd.

1692 John and Charlotte Bertrand move to Lancaster County where they purchase the 500-acre *Powell's Quarter* plantation from John Loyd for 200 pounds sterling.

1693 John Bertrand files a lawsuit to establish his possession of adjacent surplus land along Deep Creek.

1694 In March, Lancaster County justices, led by Robert "King" Carter, rule against John Bertrand in the Deep Creek surplus land case.

1696 John Loyd sues John Bertrand for the 134 pounds sterling that he still owes for the plantation.

1698 In October, John Bertrand secures a new grant from the

Northern Neck Proprietary through its agent, William Fitzhugh, resolving the four-and-a-half year legal struggle for control of the disputed surplus acres and expanding Bertrand's plantation from 500 acres to 924 acres.

1701 In July or August, John Bertrand dies, and is most likely buried at his plantation. His will entails the plantation, bequeaths it to his 13-year old son William, and designates Charlotte to manage it until William is of age.

1703 John Loyd sues Charlotte Bertrand for the 66 pounds sterling she still owes for the plantation that is becoming known as *Deep Creek*, where she is developing a store and tobacco trading business.

1709 Charlotte's daughter, Mary Ann, marries Charles Ewell in Lancaster County. They will have five children born at the Deep Creek plantation: Mary Ann (born c. 1710), Charles (c.1712—1747), Charlotte (c. 1714—c. 1782), Bertrand (c. 1716—1794), and Solomon (c. 1718—1767).

1712 In December, Charlotte Bertrand surrenders 125 acres of her one-third widow's interest in the *Deep Creek* plantation to her son William. This tract encompasses her plantation home. The following day, William Bertrand leases the same 125 acres and Charlotte's home to his brother-in-law Charles Ewell.

1713 William Bertrand marries Susanna Foushee, daughter of close Bertrand friends and fellow Huguenot refugees James and Mary Foushee, with whom he will have one surviving child at *Deep Creek*: Mary Ann (1717-1770).

1719 Charles Ewell renews his lease of 125 acres of the plantation at D*eep Creek*. The lease to the Ewells eventually grows to 225 acres so that Charlotte's son and daughter are effectively sharing the plantation.

1721 In February or March, Charlotte Bertrand dies.

1722 In February or March, Charles Ewell dies leaving his widow with five children age 12 and under. In October, William Bertrand is sworn in by Lancaster County justices as tobacco receiver for Deep Creek, thereby strengthening the family tobacco trading business.

1724 In December, Mary Ann Bertrand Ewell marries William Ballandine in Lancaster County. They will have two children born at *Deep Creek*: Frances (c. 1728–1792), and Hannah (c. 1730–c. 1770).

1726 In January, George (an enslaved bricklayer belonging to William Ballandine) is tried for the murder of Harry (a slave belonging to William Bertrand) and found guilty of manslaughter.

1734 Mary Ann Bertrand (daughter of William Bertrand) marries Leroy Griffin of Richmond County. Mary Ann and Leroy will have eight children at the Griffin plantation in Richmond County: Thomas Bertrand (1735–1778), Elizabeth (born 1737), Leroy (1738–1775), Corbin (1741–1813), William (born 1743), Samuel (1746–1810), Cyrus (1748–1810), and John Tayloe (born 1750).

1736 In June or July, William Ballandine dies.

1739 After growing up at the *Deep Creek* plantation, four of Mary Ann Bertrand Ballandine's children (Charles

Ewell, Jr., Bertrand Ewell, Charlotte Ewell Gallahue, and Frances Ballandine) and two of her step-children (William and John Ballandine) move to Prince William County where they establish a store and tobacco trading business in the port town of Dumfies.

1742 Mary Ann Bertrand Ballandine marries James Ball (first cousin of Mary Ball, mother of George Washington). This marriage along with the marriages of Mary Ann's sons (Charles Ewell Jr. and Solomon Ewell) to the daughters of James Ball (Sarah and Eve) confirm the family's position among the Lancaster County gentry.

1750 In February, Mary Ann Bertrand Ball dies and is buried at St. Mary's Whitechapel cemetery. Bertrand Ewell and the heirs of Charles Ewell, Jr. form "Ewell and Company" to acquire more than 4,500 acres in Prince William County and begin leasing it to John Ballandine who is developing an iron works.

1760 John Ballandine loses investors and faces financial ruin. To protect the *Deep Creek* plantation from the Ballandine/"Ewell and Company" creditors, William Bertrand signs a tripartite deed in July, placing his estate in the hands of the wealthy Charles Carter (grandson of "King" Carter) to be delivered to his grandson, Thomas Bertrand Griffin, after William's death.

1761 William Bertrand dies in February or March, and the *Deep Creek* plantation is subsequently delivered into the ownership of Thomas Bertrand Griffin, who names the plantation *Belle Isle*.

1766 Thomas Bertrand Griffin marries Judith Burwell, daughter of Carter Burwell and great-granddaughter of Robert "King" Carter.

1767 Thomas Bertrand Griffin and Judith Griffin build a stylish Georgian home at *Belle Isle* that was likely influenced by the impressive mansion her father built 12 years earlier at Carter's Grove near Williamsburg.

1769 Judith Burwell Griffin dies leaving no surviving children.

1771 Thomas Bertrand Griffin is appointed Clerk of the Lancaster County Court. In England to pursue legal studies, Thomas' brother Cyrus elopes with Lady Christina Stuart, daughter of John Stuart, Earl of Traquair.

1775 In the spring, Cyrus and Lady Christina Griffin sail from England to Virginia where they apparently assume temporary residence at *Belle Isle*.

1776 On July 18, Thomas Bertrand Griffin and the court justices of Lancaster County swear allegiance to the new commonwealth, signifying that they no longer serve the British king.

1777 In March, Thomas Bertrand Griffin gives the 75-acre Newby tract and house, located adjacent to *Belle Isle*, to his brother Cyrus.

1778 Thomas Bertrand Griffin dies in March or April and leaves *Belle Isle* to his brother Corbin.

1782 In February, Corbin Griffin sells *Belle Isle* to Ralph Wormeley IV of *Rosegill* for 5,000 pounds cash, thereby ending 90 years of Bertrand family ownership of the plantation. Wormeley is acquiring the plantation for his daughter Mary and her husband Nathaniel Burwell.

***Belle Isle* Plantation House from a Civil War Era Sketch**
Courtesy, Mary Ball Washington Museum and Library
Lancaster, Virginia Historical Society

Appendix B: Family Trees

Powell Family Tree in Virginia
From Thomas Powell

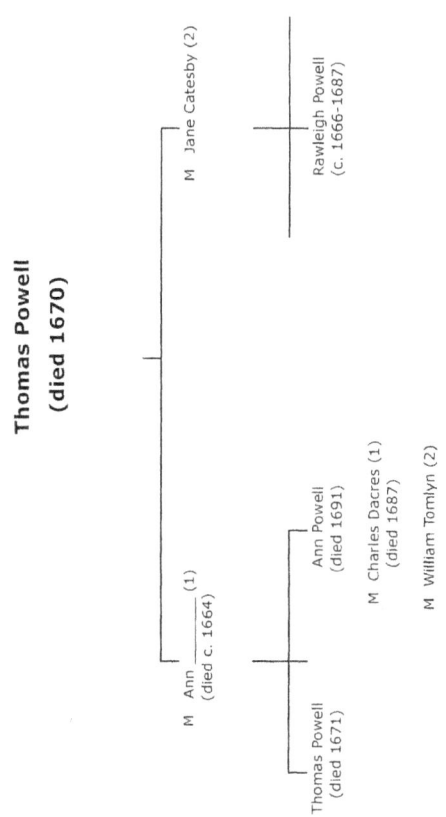

Kyrby Family Tree in Virginia
From John Kyrby

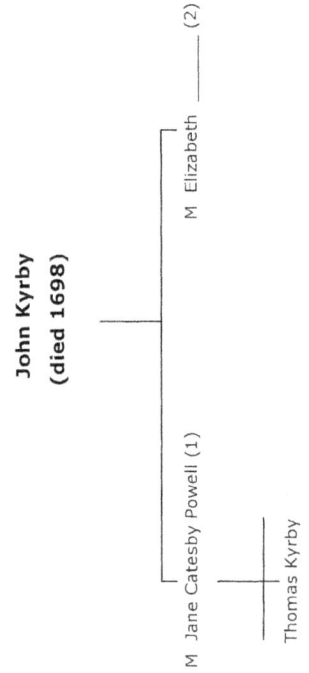

Bertrand Family Tree in France, England, and Virginia
From the Reverend N. Bertrand

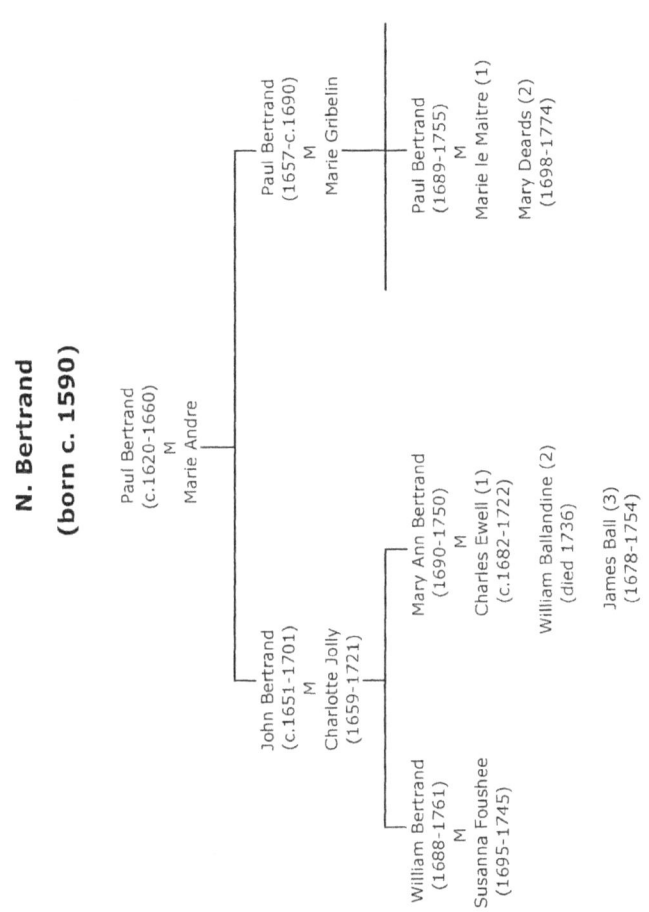

Bertrand Family Tree in Virginia
From William Bertrand

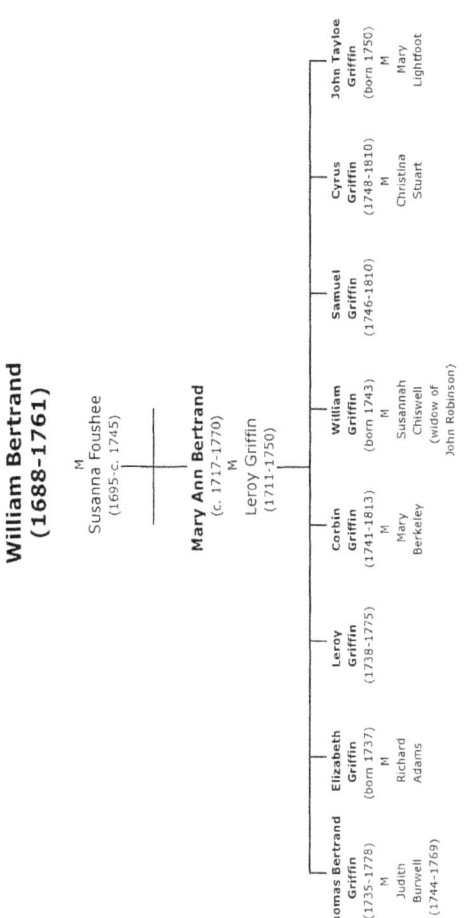

Bertrand Family Tree in Virginia
From Mary Ann Bertrand

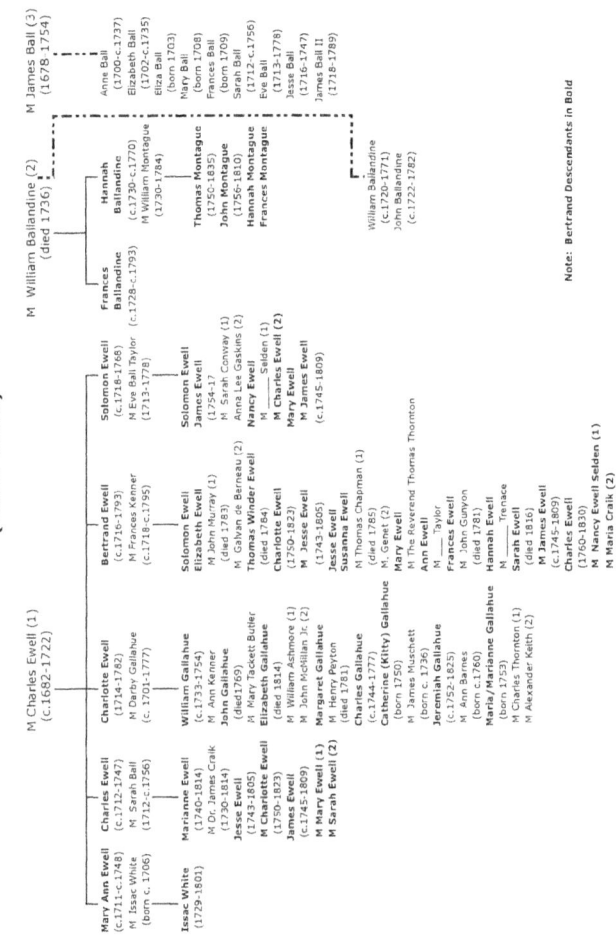

Jolly de Chadignac Family Tree in France
From Jean Jacques Jolly, Seigneur de Chadignac

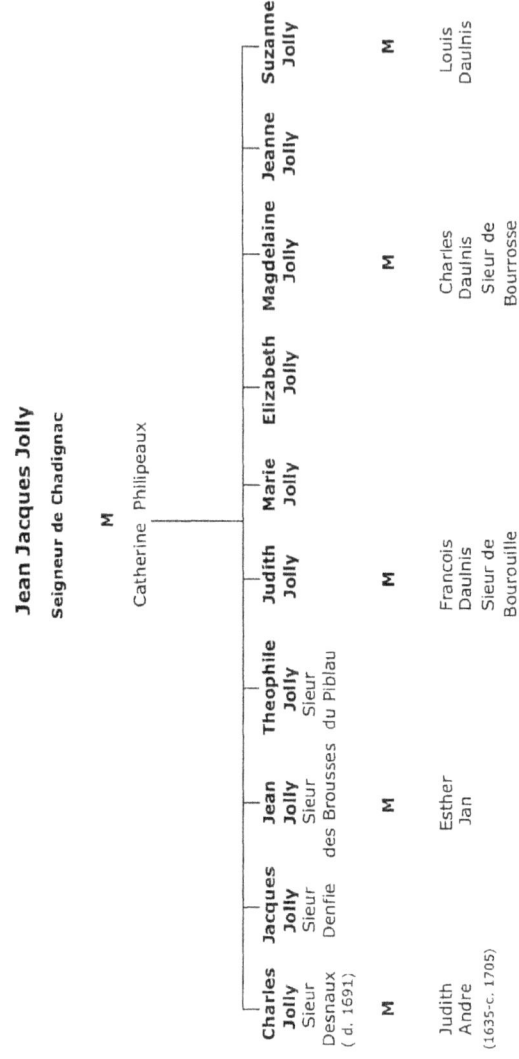

Andre Family in France
From Abraham Andre

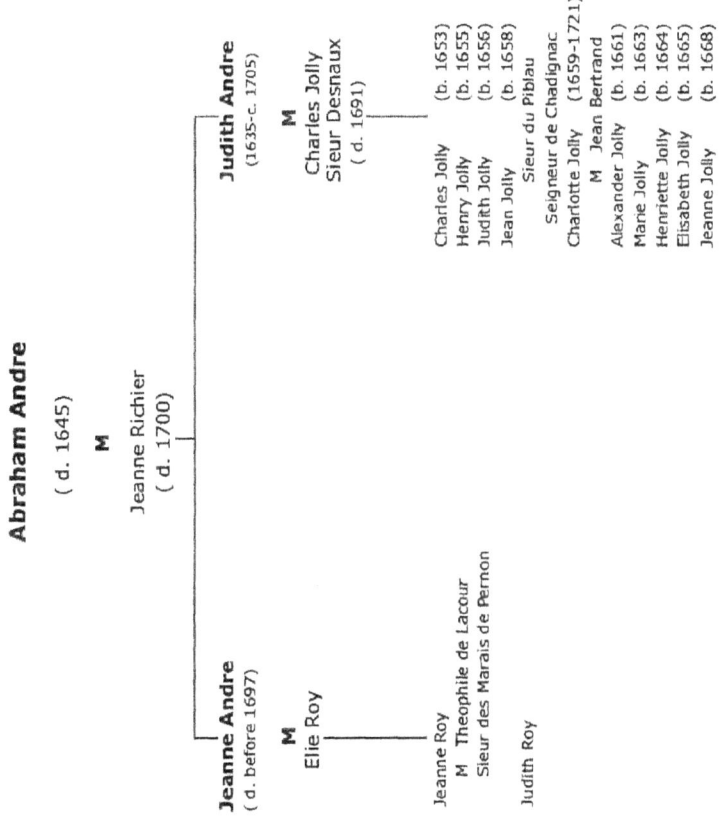

Andre Family Tree in France
From Jehan Andre

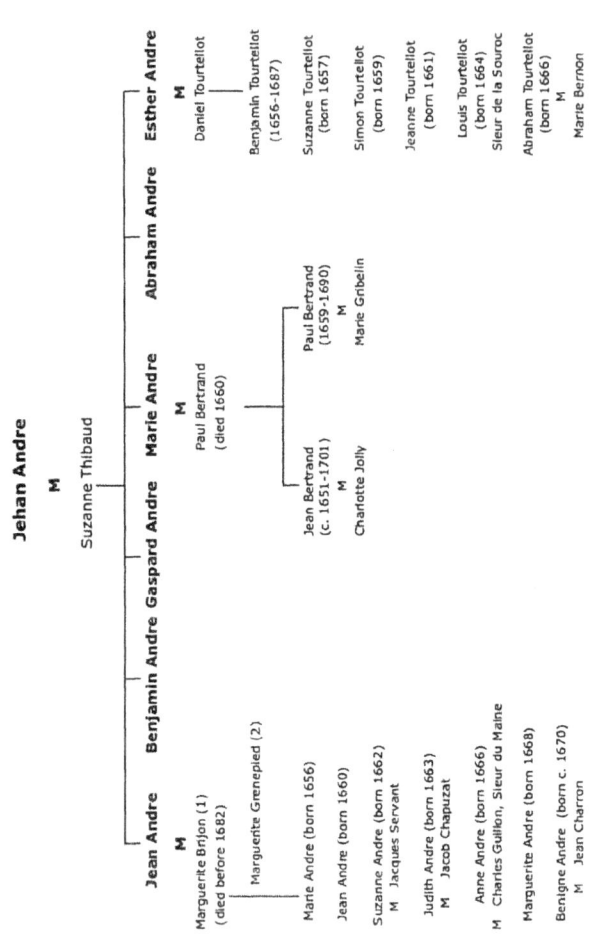

Documentation Summary of Family Trees

Powell Family Tree in Virginia from Thomas Powell:
- Chapters Two and Three.

Kyrby Family Tree in Virginia from John Kyrby:
- Chapters Two and Three.

Bertrand Family Tree in France, England, and Virginia from N. Bertrand:
- Chapters Four and Five.
- Lee, "The Transatlantic Legacy of the Protestant Church of Cozes," 36-54.

Bertrand Family Tree in Virginia from William Bertrand:
- Chapters Five through Eight.
- King, Msslk5823a, Virginia Historical Society Library, Richmond.

Bertrand Family Tree in Virginia from Mary Ann Bertrand:
- Chapters Five through Eight.
- King, Msslk5823a, Virginia Historical Society Library, Richmond.
- Hayden, *A Genealogy of the Glassell Family*, 334-342.
- Mary Lester Hill, "Ball Families of Virginia's Northern Neck," Mary Ball Washington Library, Lancaster, Virginia.

Jolly de Chadignac Family Tree in France from Jean Jacques Jolly:
- Chapter Four.
- Lee, "The Transatlantic Legacy of the Protestant Church of Cozes," 36-54.
- I-43, ADCMLR.

- C224, ADCMLR.
- File for Daulnis Famille, G 34/D2, Bibliotheque de la Société de l'Histoire Du Protestantisme Français Paris.

Andre Family Tree in France from Jehan Andre:
- Chapter Four.
- Lee, "The Transatlantic Legacy of the Protestant Church of Cozes," 36-54.
- I-43, ADCMLR.
- C224, ADCMLR.

Andre Family Tree in France from Abraham Andre:
- Chapter Four.
- Lee, "The Transatlantic Legacy of the Protestant Church of Cozes," 36-54.
- I-43, ADCMLR.
- C224, ADCMLR.

1660 Baptism Record of Charlotte Jolly Bertrand
Cozes Protestant Baptism Register
Courtesy, Archives de la Departmentales Charente-Maritime, I-43
La Rochelle, France

Bibliography

Manuscript Sources

Accomack County, Virginia Archives, Accomac, Virginia.

    Accomac County Order Book, 1676-1678.

    Accomac County Order Book, 1667-1670,

    Accomac County Wills (1692-1715), 347 (Will of James Ewell).

Archives de la Departmentales Charentes-Maritime La Rochelle, France.

    C224, Ch. Dangibeaud, *Minutes de Notaires.*

    I-43, Papiers des Baptêmes de l'Eglise Reformee de Cozes . . . Fevrier 1656-Juillet 1668.

    Notaire Bargignac, 3E, 128/52, folio 143-144.

    Notaire Tourneur, 3E, 26/1086, folio 244-245.

Canterbury Cathedral Archives, Canterbury, U.K.

    PRC 17/84/24 (Will of Edward Ewell).

Colonial Williamsburg Digital Library, Virginia Gazette.

    Pinkney, January 12, 1775, 3.

    Purdie, November 10, 1775, 2.

    Purdie, August 9, 1776, 2.

    Purdie, August 30, 1776, 3.

    Rind, November 30, 1769, 2.

    Dixon and Hunter, May 8, 1778, 7.

Guildhall Library, London.

    John Bertrand Ordination Record #9535/3.

Huguenot Library, University College, London.
> Royal Bounty, Ms 1 (Bertrand).
> Royal Bounty, Ms 1, folio 88 (Joly).

Huntington Library, San Marino, California.
> Fairfax Papers, BR Box 227 (2), folio 16.
> Fairfax Papers, White Chapel Parish Rental Roll for 1750, Box 7, BR Box 233.

Lancaster County, Virginia Archives, Lancaster, Virginia.
> *Lancaster County Deeds, Etc, Volume 7, 1687-1700.*
> *Lancaster County Order Book 1.*
> *Lancaster County Will Book, Volume 5.*
> *Lancaster, County Wills, Etc, Volume 5, 1674-1689.*
> *Lancaster County Will Book 8, 1690-1709*, 105-105a (Will of John Bertrand).
> *Lancaster County Deed Book 9, 1701-1706.*
> *Lancaster County Order Book 5, 1702-1713.*
> *Lancaster County Order Book 7, 1721-1729.*
> *Lancaster County Will Book 10*, 1709-1727, 376-378 (Will of Charles Ewell).
> *Lancaster County Deed Book 11, 1714-1728.*
> *Lancaster County Deed and Will Book 12*, 1726-1736.
> Lancaster County Register of Marriages, 16 December, 1724.
> *Lancaster County Will and Deed Book 13, 1736-1743*, 21-22 (Will of William Ballandine).
> *Lancaster Deed and Will Book 14, 1743-1750.*
> *Lancaster County Will Book 16, 1758-1763*
> > Tripartite Deed for Belle Isle, 105-106.

William Bertrand's Will, 148-149.

Lancaster County Order Book 12, 1764-1767.

Lancaster County, Virginia Deed Book 19, 1770-1782.

Lancaster County Will Book 20, folio 120 (Will of Thomas Bertrand Griffin).

Lancaster County Deed Book 21, 1782-1793.

Library of Virginia, Richmond.

    Land Office Patents no. 2, 1643-1651, 288.

    Land Office Patents no. 4, 1655-1664, 223.

    Loose Wills (Will of Thomas Powell).

    Northern Neck Grants, no. 2, 1694-1700, 293-295.

    Original Correspondence—Secretaries of State, Miscellaneous, 1771-1776, Griffin, Cyrus—1776, SR 00559.

    Commission Charles Ewell, 1778, June 1 # 44385.

    Bounty Records, Pension Application of Corbin Griffin (R-56), Correspondence between John H. Smith and Virginia Governor John B. Floyd on August 22, 1850 and September 14, 1850.

    Revolutionary War Bounty Warrants, Reels 1-29, Certificate Issued by Daniel Morgan, #44385.

    Cornwallis Papers: America, Correspondence on Exchanges of Prisoners, etc., 1781-1782, 2-3, #44862.

    Revolutionary War Bounty Warrants, Reels 1-29.

    Virginia Board of War, Samuel Griffin . . . # 44393.

    Virginia, General Assembly, Senate. Letter and Testimony of Charles Ewell, 1825, Feb. 1, # 44862.

London Metropolitan Archives, London.
> Household of Louis Casimir de la Rochefoucauld, Sieur de Fontruet; November 29, 1681, MR/R/R/032/08.

Mary Ball Washington Library, Lancaster, Virginia.
> Lancaster County Individual Tithables, 1653-1720.
> Mary Lester Hill. "Ball Families of Virginia's Northern Neck."

Prince William County, Virginia Archives, Manassas, Virginia.
> *Prince William County Deed Book D.*

Richmond County, Virginia Archives, Warsaw, Virginia.
> *Old Rappahannock County Order Book 2, 1686-1692.*

United States Congress.
> *Biographical directory of the United States Congress, 1774—present,* Griffin, Cyrus (1748-1810) [Washington D. C.: United States Congress, 1998].

Virginia Historical Society Library, Richmond.
> George Harrison Sanford King, Msslk5823a.

Published Primary Sources

Berkeley, Edmund, Jr., ed. *The Diary, Correspondence, and Papers of Robert "King" Carter of Virginia, 1701-1732.* Robert Carter to John Pemberton, January 28, 1723/24. http//www.christchurch1735.org.

Beverley, Robert. *The History and Present State of Virginia,* ed., Louis B. Wright. Chapel Hill, NC: University of North Carolina Press, 1947.

Boyd, Julian P. ed. *The Papers of Thomas Jefferson* 16, 30 November—4 July 1790. Princeton, NJ: Princeton University Press, 1961.

Crozier, William Armstrong, ed. *Virginia County Records 2, Virginia County Militia, 1651-1776.* Baltimore: Genealogical Publishing Company, 1905.

Davis, Richard Beale ed. *William Fitzhugh and His Chesapeake World 1676-1701: The Fitzhugh Letters and Other Documents.* Chapel Hill: North Carolina University Press, 1963.

Dorman, John Frederick.
Prince William County, Virginia Will Book C, 1733-1744. Washington, DC: Printed by the Author, 1956.
Virginia Revolutionary Pension Applications 35. Washington, DC: Printed by the Author, 1958.

Fleet, Beverley. *Virginia Colonial Abstracts,* vol. 1. Baltimore: Genealogical Publishing Company, 1961.

Headley, Robert K., ed. *Married Well and Often: Marriages of the Northern Neck of Virginia, 1649-1800.* Baltimore: Genealogical Publishing Company, 2003.

Hening, William Walter, ed. *Statutes at Large: Being a Collection of All the Laws of Virginia, vols. 6 and 9,* New York, 1821.

Hening, William Waller, and Samuel Shepherd, eds. *The Statutes at Large of Virginia from October 1792 to December 1806,* vol. 1. Richmond, VA, 1835-36.

Hillman, Benjamin J., ed. *Executive Journals of the Council of Virginia*, vol. 6, June 20, 1754—May 3, 1775. Richmond, VA: Virginia State Library, 1966.

Hopkins, William Lindsay, ed. *Isle of Wight County, Virginia Deeds, 1647-1710, Court Orders, 1693-1695, and Guardian Accounts, 1740-1767.* Athens, GA: New Papyrus Publishing, 1994.

Hutchinson, Richard S. *Lancaster County, Virginia Abstracts of Order Book 8, Part One, 1728-1737.* Millsboro, DE: Colonial Roots, 2014.

Lancaster County, Virginia Abstracts of Wills, Administrations, Deeds, Inventories, Etc., 1726-1735. Berwyn Heights, MD: Heritage Press, 2011.

Jefferson, Isaac. "Life of Isaac Jefferson of Petersburg, Virginia, Blacksmith (1847)." *Encyclopedia Virginia*, Virginia Humanities, May 3, 2013.

Kilby, Craig M., ed. *Lancaster County, Virginia Will Book 10, 1709-1727.* Athens, GA: New Papyrus Publishing, 2014.

King, George Harrison Sanford, ed. *The Register of Overwharton Parish, Stafford County, Virginia, 1723-1758, and Sundry Historical and Genealogical Notes.* Fredricksburg, VA: Printed by the Author, 1961.

_____. *The Registers of North Farnham Parish, 1663-1814 and Lunenburg Parish, 1783-1800, Richmond County, Virginia.* Fredericksburg, VA: Printed by the Author, 1966.

Manassas Journal Messenger. Centennial Edition (1969), Prince William County, RELIC Digital Library.

McKey, JoAnn Riley. *Accomac County, Virginia Court Order Abstracts, 1703-1710,* vol. 10. Berwyn Heights, MD: Heritage Books, 2001.

_____. *Accomac County, Virginia Court Order Abstracts, 1710-1714,* vol. 11. Berwyn Heights, MD: Heritage Books, 2001.

Nugent, Nell, M. *Cavaliers and Pioneers, A Calendar of Virginia Land Grants, 1623-1800,* vol. 1. Richmond, VA: Press of the Dietz Printing Company, 1934.

Palmer, William P., ed. *Calendar of Virginia State Papers and Other Manuscripts, 1652-1781,* vol. 7. Richmond, VA, 1875.

Peters, Joan W. *Prince William County, Virginia Patriots and Pensioners, 1752-1856.* Berwyn Heights, MD: Heritage Books, 2010.

Sparacio, Ruth and Sam Sparacio. *Lancaster County Deed and Will Book, 1654-1661.* McLean, VA: Antient Press, 1991.

_____. *Lancaster County Order Book, 1656-1661.* McLean, VA: Antient Press, 1993.

_____. *Lancaster County Order Book, 1662-1666.* McLean, VA: Antient Press, 1993.

_____. *Lancaster County Deed and Will Book, 1661-1702.* McLean, VA: Antient Press, 1991.

_____. *Lancaster County Order Book, 1670-1674.* McLean, VA: Antient Press, 1993.

_____. *Lancaster County Order Book, 1682-1687.* McLean, VA: Antient Press, 1995.

_____. *Lancaster County Order Book, 1687-1691.* McLean, VA: Antient Press, 1995.

_____. *Lancaster County Order Book, 1691-1695.* McLean, VA: Antient Press, 1995.

_____. *Lancaster County Order Book, 1695-1699.* McLean, VA: Antient Press, 1995.

_____. *Lancaster County Order Book, 1699-1701.* McLean, VA: Antient Press, 1998.

_____. *Lancaster County Deed Book, 1701-1706.* McLean, VA: Antient Press, 1995.

_____. *Lancaster County Deed Book, 1706-1710.* McLean, VA: Antient Press, 1995.

_____. *Lancaster County Order Book, 1729-1743.* McLean, VA: Antient Press, 1998.

_____. Old *Rappahannock County Order Book, 1685-1687.* McLean, VA: Antient Press, 1990.

_____. *Old Rappahannock County Order Book, 1689-1692.* McLean, VA: Antient Press, 1990.

_____. *Deed Abstracts of Prince William County, 1749-1752/1761-1764.* McLean, VA: Antient Press, 1989.

The Huguenot (Founders of Manakin), no. 11 (1941-1943).

The Virginia Magazine of History and Biography 1, no. 3 (January 1894), 254-256.

_____ 8, no. 3 (January 1901), 308.

_____ 19, no. 4 (October 1911), 417.

_____ 49, no. 1 (February 2011), 49-50.

Twohig, Dorothy, ed. *The Papers of George Washington, Presidential Series,* vol. 4, 8 September 1789—15 January 1790, Charlottesville, VA: University Press of Virginia, 1993.

Tupper, Margaret H., ed. *Christ Church Parish, Lancaster County, Virginia Vestry Book, 1739-1786.* Irvington, VA: Foundation for Historic Christ Church, 1990.

United States Senate. *The Pension Roll of 1835.* Baltimore: Genealogical Publishing Company, 1992.

Secondary Sources

Bosher, J. F. "Huguenot Merchants and the Protestant International in the Seventeenth Century." *The William and Mary Quarterly* 52 (January 1995): 77-102.

Carlo, Paula Wheeler. *Huguenot Refugees in Colonial New York: Becoming American in the Hudson Valley.* Brighton, UK: Sussex Academic Press, 2005.

Casdorph, Paul D. *Confederate General R. S. Ewell: Robert E. Lee's Hesitant Commander.* Lexington: University Press of Kentucky, 2004.

Davis, Richard Beale. *Intellectual life in the Colonial South, 1585-1763.* Knoxville: University of Tennessee Press, 1978.

Dowdey, Clifford. *The Virginia Dynasties: The Emergence of "King" Carter and the Golden Age.* Boston: Little, Brown, 1969.

Freeman, Douglas Southall. *Young Washington,* v ol. I, Appendix I-1. New York: Charles Scribner's Sons, 1948.

Fuchs, Ron. Unpublished paper delivered to the Association for the Preservation of Virginia Antiquities on March 18, 2004.

Gentry, Daphne, and the Dictionary of Virginia Biography. "Carter Burwell (1716-1756)." *Encyclopedia Virginia*, Virginia Humanities, August 21, 2014.

Harrison, Fairfax. *Landmarks of Old Prince William*. Baltimore: Gateway Press, 1987.

Hatfield, April Lee. *Atlantic Virginia: Intercolonial Relationships in the Seventeenth Century*. Philadelphia: University of Pennsylvania Press, 2004.

Hayden, Horace Edwin. *A Genealogoy of the Glassell Family of Scotland and Virginia*. Wilkes-Barre, PA, 1891.

Horn, James. *Adapting to a New World: English Society in the Seventeenth-Century Chesapeake*. Chapel Hill: University of North Carolina Press, 1994.

Isaac, Rhys. *The Transformation of Virginia, 1740-1790*. Chapel Hill: University of North Carolina Press, 1999.

James River Institute for Archeology, Inc. *Phase I Archeological Survey of Belle Isle, Lancaster County, Virginia*. Jamestown, VA, 1992.

Jett, Carolyn H. *Lancaster County, Virginia: Where the River Meets the Bay*. Lancaster, VA: The Lancaster County History Book Committee, 2003.

Kilby, Craig M. "Did You Know Slaves Were Real Property." Mary Ball Washington History and Research Center Newsletter 1, issue 2, (November 2015).

Lee, Lonnie H. "The Transatlantic Legacy of the Protestant Church of Cozes." *The Huguenot Society Journal* 32 (2019): 36-54.

Neale, Elizabeth Lewis. "St. Mary's Whitechapel, Lancaster County, Virginia." In *Colonial Churches: A Series of Sketches in the Original Colony of Virginia,* edited by W. M. Clarke, 308-312, Richmond, VA: Southern Churchman,1907.

Nicolson, Joseph, and Richard Burn. *The History and Antiquities of the Counties of Westmoreland and Cumberland*, vol. 2. London, 1777.

Rorer, Henry S. "Cyrus Griffin: Virginia's First Federal Judge." *Washington and Lee Law Review* 21, issue 2, article 4, (September 1, 1964): 201-214.

Rouse, Parke. *James Blair of Virginia.* Chapel Hill: University of North Carolina Press, 1971.

Salmon, Emily Jones, and John Salmon. "Tobacco in Colonial Virginia." *Encyclopedia Virginia*, Virginia Humanities, January 29, 2013.

Tarter, Brent. "Evidence of Religion in Seventeenth Century Virginia." In *From Jamestown to Jefferson: The Evolution of Religious Freedom in Virginia,* edited by Paul Rasor and Richard E. Bond, 17-37, Charlottesville: University of Virginia Press, 2011.

Tilson, Albert, and the Dictionary of Virginia Biography. "Charles Carter (1732-1806)." *Encyclopedia Virginia*, Virginia Humanities, April 19, 2017.

Warner, Thomas Hoskins. *History of Old Rappahannock County, 1656-1692.* Tappahannock, VA: P. P. Warner, 1965.

Wells, Camille, "Belle Isle." Unpublished essay, 2014.

Wheeler, Robert A. *Lancaster County, Virginia, 1650-1750: The Evolution of a Southern Tidewater Community.* Providence, RI: Brown University Phd. Dissertation, 1972.

William and Mary Center for Archeological Research. William H. Moore, David W. Lewes, and Joe B. Jones. *Archeological Evaluation of Sites 44LA147 and 44LA175, Belle Isle State Park, Lancaster County, Virginia.* Williamsburg, VA, 2006.

Annotated Index of Names

Names followed by * designate residents of *Belle Isle* Plantation between 1650 and 1782.

Abraham* (James Foushee will), 66

Adam* (Thomas Bertrand Griffin inventory), 92

Adams, Richard, 120

Anderson, Comfort, 58

Anderson, Naomi, 58

Anderson, William, 58

Andre, Abraham (grandfather of Charlotte Bertrand), 28, 124

Andre, Abraham, 123

Andre, Anne, 123

Andre, Benigne, 123

Andre, Benjamin, 123

Andre, Esther, 123

Andre, Gaspard, 123

Andre, Jean, Sr., 123

Andre, Jean, Jr., 123

Andre, Jeanne, 124

Andre, Jehan, 123

Andre, Judith (mother of Charlotte Bertrand) 28, 45, 122, 124

Andre, Judith, 123

Andre, Marguerite, 123

Andre, Marie (wife of Paul Bertrand, Sr.), 28, 123

Andre, Marie, 123

Andre, Suzanne, 123

Anthony* (Thomas Bertrand Griffin inventory), 92

Arnold, Benedict, 100

Ashmore, William, 121

Ball, Anne, 121

Ball, Eliza, 121

Ball, Elizabeth, 121

Ball, Eve, 69, 112

Ball, Frances, 121

Ball, Jesse, 121

Ball, James, Sr., 70, 72, 112, 119, 121

Ball, James, Jr., 121

Ball, Mary (mother of George Washington), 112

Ball, Mary, 121

Ball, Mary Ann* (nee Bertrand), 70-73, 112

Ball, Sarah, 70, 73, 112, 121

Ball, William, 70

Ballandine, Frances,* 65, 73, 111-112, 121

Ballandine, Hannah,* 65, 70, 111, 121

Ballandine, John,* 65, 73, 100, 112, 121

Ballandine, Mary Ann* (nee Bertrand), 69-70, 100, 112

Ballandine, William Sr.,* 64-68, 70, 111, 119, 121

Ballandine, William Jr.,* 65, 73, 112, 121

Barnes, Ann, 121

Ben* (boy—Charles Ewell will and inventory), 68

Berkeley, Mary, 120

Bernon, Marie, 123

Bertrand, Charlotte* (nee Jolly), 32, 33, 41-55, 57, 60-63, 69, 81, 97, 100, 108-110, 127

Bertrand, John* (the Reverend), ix, 27-37, 39, 41-43, 48, 52-53, 55, 57, 63, 69, 81, 97, 100, 108-109, 119, 123-124

Bertrand, Mary Ann* (daughter of John Bertrand), 29, 35, 42-43, 52, 57, 59, 109, 119, 121

Bertrand, Mary Ann* (daughter of William Bertrand), 63, 110-111, 120

Bertrand, N. (the Reverend), 27, 119

Bertrand, Paul, Sr. (the Reverend), 27, 119, 123

Bertrand, Paul, Jr. (the Reverend), 53, 119, 123

Bertrand, Paul III, 42, 53, 119

Bertrand, Susannah* (nee Foushee), 63, 66

Bertrand, William,* 29, 41-43, 49, 57, 60-65, 67-69, 72-76, 79, 83, 109-113, 119-120

Beth* (Thomas Bertrand Griffin inventory), 92

Betty* (woman—Charles Ewell inventory), 68

Betty* (girl—Charles Ewell inventory inventory), 68

Betty* (William Bertrand inventory), 76

Betty* (William Bertrand inventory), 76

Betty* (Thomas Bertrand Griffin inventory), 92

Beverley, Robert, 53-54

Biley* (James Foushee will), 66

Billey* (William Bertrand inventory), 76

Billy* (Thomas Bertrand Griffin inventory), 92

Braddock, Edward, 98

Brassier, Jeffrey* (servant of John Bertrand), 35

Brent, George, 39

Brijon, Marguerite, 123

Bricker* (William Ballandine inventory), 68

Brissot de Warville, Pierre, 101

Bristow* (boy—Charles Ewell inventory), 68

Bristow* (boy—Charles Ewell inventory), 68

Bristol* (William Ballandine inventory), 68

Browne, Nathaniel, 17, 22

Burwell, Carter, 80, 113

Burwell, Judith,* 80, 113, 120

Burwell, Mary (nee Wormley), 103

Burwell, Nathaniel (son-in-law of Ralph Wormley IV), 103, 114

Burwell, Nathaniel (uncle of Judith Burwell Griffin), 103

Burwell, Robert, 103

Butler, Mary Tackett, 121

Caeser* (man—Charles Ewell Inventory), 68

Carter, Charles, 74-75, 113

Carter, Robert "King," 33-34, 65, 74, 80, 103, 108, 113

Cate* (William Ballandine inventory), 68

Catesby, Jane,* 11-12, 18, 107, 117-118

Cato* (William Bertrand inventory), 76

Chapman, Thomas, 121

Chapuzat, Jacob, 123

Charles* (James Foushee will), 66

Charles* (William Bertrand inventory) 76

Charles* (Thomas Bertrand Griffin inventory), 92

Charles* (Thomas Bertrand Griffin inventory), 92

Charles II, (king of England), 34

Charron, Jean, 123

Chiswell, Susannah, 120

Comfort* (Charles Ewell will and inventory), 68

Conway, Sarah, 121

Cooper, Thomas, 51

Cornwallis, Charles Lord Cornwallis, (1st Marquess Cornwallis), 95

Craik, Dr. James, 98, 121

Craik, Maria, 121

Criss* (William Bertrand inventory), 76

Criss* (Thomas Bertrand Griffin inventory) 92

Dacres, Ann* (nee Powell), 19, 21, 108

Dacres, Charles, 19, 21, 117

Dan* (William Bertrand inventory), 76

Dan* (Thomas Bertrand Griffin inventory), 92

Daniel* (William Bertrand inventory), 76

Daulnis, Charles (Sieur de Bourrosse), 122

Daulnis, Francois (Sieur de Bourouille), 122

Daulnis, Louis, 122

David* (Thomas Bertrand Griffin inventory), 92

Davie* (William Ballandine inventory), 68

Deards, Mary, 119

Deinne, Eleanor* (servant of John Bertrand), 35, 36

de Berneau, Galvan, 121

de Lacour, Theophile (Sieur des Marais de Pernon), 124

de Lafayette, Marquis, 99

de la Rochefoucauld, Louis Casimir (Sieur de Fontruet), 27

Dick* (James Foushee will), 66

Dick* (Thomas Bertrand Griffin inventory), 92

Dobson, Charles, 44

Doly* (John Bertrand will), 35

Doming* (William Bertrand inventory), 76

Doming* (Thomas Bertrand Griffin inventory), 55

Downman, Rawleigh, 103

Duke* (William Ballandine inventory), 68

DuPont, Henry Francis, 81

Elijah* (Thomas Bertrand Griffin inventory), 92

Ellin* (Thomas Bertrand Griffin inventory), 92

Ewell, Ann, 121

Ewell, Bertrand,* (son of Charles Ewell, Sr.), 63, 73, 74, 98, 109, 112, 121

Ewell, Charles, Sr.,* 57-64, 67-68, 71, 74, 109-110, 119, 121

Ewell, Charles, Jr.,* 63, 70, 73, 97-98, 109, 112, 121

Ewell, Charles (son of Bertrand Ewell), 99, 121

Ewell, Charlotte,* (daughter of Charles Ewell, Sr.), 63, 109, 121

Ewell, Charlotte, 121

Ewell, Edward, 58

Ewell, Elizabeth, 121

Ewell, Frances, 121

Ewell, Hannah, 121

Ewell, James (father of Charles Ewell, Sr.), 58

Ewell, James (son of Charles, Jr.), 97, 121

Ewell, James (son of Solomon Ewell), 99, 121

Ewell, Jesse (son of Charles Ewell, Jr.), 97, 121

Ewell, Jesse, 121

Ewell, Marianne (daughter of Charles Ewell, Jr.), 98, 121

Ewell, Mark, 58

Ewell, Mary, 121

Ewell, Mary, 121

Ewell, Mary Ann* (nee Bertrand), 62-65, 71, 109, 111

Ewell, Mary Ann* (daughter of Charles Ewell, Sr.), 62, 63, 121

Ewell, Nancy, 121

Ewell, Sarah, 121

Ewell, Solomon (brother of Charles Ewell, Sr.), 58

Ewell, Solomon* (son of Charles Ewell, Sr.), 63, 70, 73, 99, 109, 112, 121

Ewell, Solomon, 121

Ewell, Solomon, 121

Ewell, Susannah, 121

Ewell, Thomas Winder (son of Bertrand Ewell), 99, 121

Fillis* (James Foushee will), 66

Fillis* (girl in James Foushee will), 66

Fill* (William Ballandine inventory), 68

Fitzhugh, Henry,* 32

Fitzhugh, William, Sr., 30-32, 33-34, 39

Fitzhugh, William, Jr.,* 29

Fletcher, William, 51

Fortune* (man—Charles Ewell inventory), 68

Fortune* (William Ballandine inventory), 68

Fortune* (William Bertrand inventory), 76

Foushee, James,* 43, 63, 65-66, 110

Foushee, John, 66

Foushee, Marie, 63, 110

Foushee, Ruth,* 66

Foushee, Susannah,* 63, 110, 119-120

Foushee, William, 66

Fox, David, 12

Fox, William, 48-49

Frank* (William Bertrand inventory), 76

Frank* (Thomas Bertrand Griffin inventory), 92

Franklin, Benjamin, 96, 101

Fry, Joshua, 89

Furney, Robert* (servant of John Bertrand), 35

Gallahue, Catherine/Kitty, 121

Gallahue, Charles, 99, 121

Gallahue, Charlotte* (nee Ewell), 73, 99, 112

Gallahue, Darby, 73, 121

Gallahue, Elizabeth, 121

Gallahue, Jeremiah, 99, 121

Gallahue, John, 99, 121

Gallahue, Margaret, 121

Gallahue, Maria/Marianne, 121

Gallahue, William, 121

Gaskins, Anna Lee, 121

Genet, _____, 121

George* (man, enslaved brick layer —Charles Ewell will and inventory), 68, 71

George* (enslaved brick layer of William Ballandine who is found guilty of manslaughter), 68-69, 111

George III (king of England), 51

Gibson, John, 17

Grasnier* (William Bertrand inventory), 76

Grenepied, Marguerite, 123

Gribelin, Marie, 53, 119, 123

Gribelin, Simon, 53

Griffin, Christina (nee Lady Christina Stuart), 87, 101-102, 114

Griffin, Corbin, 74, 91-95, 100, 103-104, 111, 114, 120

Griffin, Cyrus,* 74, 85-87, 96-97, 100-103, 111, 113-114, 120

Griffin, Elizabeth, 74, 111, 120

Griffin, John Tayloe, 74, 111, 120

Griffin, Judith* (nee Burwell), 81-82, 103

Griffin, Leroy, Sr., 74, 111, 120

Griffin, Leroy, Jr., 74, 91, 95, 111, 120

Griffin, Mary (nee Berkeley), 95

Griffin, Mary* (daughter of Cyrus Griffin), 87

Griffin, Mary Ann* (nee Bertrand), 74, 79

Griffin, Samuel, 74, 95, 111, 120

Griffin, Thomas Bertrand,* 74-75, 79-80, 82-87, 91-92, 95, 111, 113-114, 120

Griffin, William, 74, 96, 111, 120

Guillon, Charles (Sieur de Maine), 123

Gunyan, John, 121

Hannah* (Mary Ann Bertrand Ball inventory), 71

Harry* (enslaved worker of William Bertrand who died in 1725), 68, 111

Harry* (William Bertrand inventory), 76

Harry* (Thomas Bertrand Griffin inventory), 92

Hayward, Nicholas, 31

Hector* (James Foushee will), 66

Henry, Patrick, 101

Herrman, Augustine, 20, 25

Hinde, Thomas, 51

Hole, William, 2

Hope, Comfort, 58

Howell, John* (servant of John Bertrand), 35

Jacob* (Thomas Bertrand Griffin inventory), 92

Jack* (enslaved worker of John Bertrand), 35

Jack* (William Ballandine inventory), 68

Jack* (enslaved worker of William Bertrand), 76

Jan, Esther, 122

Jefferson, Thomas, 101-102

Jefferson, Peter, 89

Jenny* (woman—Charles Ewell will and inventory), 68

Jenny* (William Ballandine inventory), 68

Jenny* (Mary Ann Bertrand Ball inventory), 71

Jenny* (William Bertrand inventory), 76

Jenny* (William Bertrand inventory), 76

Jenny* (Thomas Bertrand Griffin inventory), 92

Jimmy* (William Ballandine inventory), 68

Joe* (Charles Ewell inventory), 68

Joe* (boy—Charles Ewell will), 68

John* (enslaved boy of John Bertrand), 35

John* (Thomas Bertrand Griffin inventory), 92

John* (Thomas Bertrand Griffin inventory), 92

Jolly, Alexander, 124

Jolly, Charles, Sr. (Sieur d'Esnaux), 28, 122, 124

Jolly, Charles, Jr., 124

Jolly, Charlotte,* 28, 119, 123-124

Jolly, Elizabeth, 122

Jolly, Elizabeth (sister of Charlotte Jolly), 124

Jolly, Henry, 124

Jolly, Henriette, 124

Jolly, Jacques (Sieur Denfie), 122

Jolly, Jean Jacques (Seigneur de Chadignac), 122

Jolly, Jean (Seigneur de Chadignac), 28, 124

Jolly, Jean (Sieur de Brousses), 122

Jolly, Jeanne, 122

Jolly, Jeanne, 124

Jolly, Judith, 122

Jolly, Judith (sister of Charlotte Jolly), 124

Jolly, Magdelaine, 122

Jolly, Marie, 122

Jolly, Marie (sister of Charlotte Jolly), 124

Jolly, Suzanne, 122

Jolly, Theolphile (Sieur du Piblau), 122

Judy* (woman—Charles Ewell inventory), 68

Katy* (John Bertrand will), 35

Keith, Alexander, 121

Kenner, Ann, 121

Kenner, Frances, 73

Kyrby, Elizabeth (nee_____), 118

Kyrby, Jane* (nee Catesby), 18, 19

Kyrby, John* 18, 19, 20, 21, 22, 107-108, 118

Kirby, Thomas* 19, 118

Lawson, William* (servant of John Bertrand), 35

Lawson, William (Bristol merchant), 50-51

le Maitre, Marie, 119

Lee, Light Horse Harry, 75

Legge, William Lord Dartmouth (2nd Earl of Dartmouth), 96-97

Letty* (Charles Ewell will and inventory), 68

Liddy* (Thomas Bertrand Griffin inventory), 92

Lightfoot, Mary, 120

Lord, Owen* (servant of John Bertrand), 35

Louis XIV (king of France), 27

Loyd, John, 22, 29, 46, 108-109

Loyd, William, 21, 22, 29, 108

Mackey, Thomas, 51

Madison, James, 101

Makemie, Francis, 58

Makemie, Naomi (nee Anderson), 58

Malone, Margaret* (servant of Charles Ewell), 42

Marshall, John, 101

McMillan, John, Jr., 121

Milly* (Thomas Bertrand Griffin inventory), 92

Molly* (William Ballandine inventory), 68

Molly* (Thomas Bertrand Griffin inventory), 55

Montague, Frances, 73 121

Montague, Hannah* (nee Ballandine), 73, 100

Montague, Hannah, 121

Montague, John, 121

Montague, Thomas, 100, 121

Montague, William, 70, 73, 121

More* (William Bertrand inventory), 76

Muchleroy, Bryon* (servant of John Bertrand), 35

Murphy, Charles* (servant of William Ballandine), 68

Murray, John, 121

Muschett, James, 121

Nan* (William Bertrand inventory), 76

Nan* (Thomas Bertrand Griffin inventory), 92

Nan* (Thomas Bertrand Griffin inventory), 92

Nanny* (Charles Ewell will), 68

Nanny* (Thomas Bertrand Griffin inventory), 92

Nelson, General Thomas, Jr., 57

Newby, Henry, 83

Newby, Mary, 83

Pat* (Thomas Bertrand Griffin inventory), 92

Pemberton, John, 65

Peter* (enslaved boy of John Bertrand), 35

Peyton, Henry, 121

Philipeaux, Catherine (Charlotte Bertrand's grandmother), 60

Phillis* (Thomas Bertrand Griffin inventory), 55

Place, Francis, 7

Place, Mary, 7

Planter* (Thomas Bertrand Griffin inventory), 92

Pompey* (William Ballandine inventory), 68

Poore, Alexander* (servant of Charlotte Bertrand), 46

Poore, Eleanor* (servant of Charlotte Bertrand), 46

Poore, Frances* (servant of Charlotte Bertrand), 46

Powell, Ann* (wife of Thomas Powell, Sr.), 10-11, 117

Powell, Ann* (daughter of Thomas Powell, Sr.), 10-11, 117

Powell, Howell, 8-9

Powell, Jane* (nee Catesby), 17, 107

Powell, Rawleigh,* 17-21, 107-108, 117

Powell, Thomas, Sr.,* ix, 7-13, 15, 17-19, 33, 61, 107, 117

Powell, Thomas, Jr.,* 7-8, 10, 17-18, 107, 117

Powell, Thomas (of Old Rappahannock County), 7

Powhatan (chief of Powhatan Algonquins), 1-2

Rachel* (Thomas Bertrand Griffin inventory), 92

Rawleigh* (Thomas Bertrand Griffin inventory), 92

Rebecah* (James Foushee will), 66

Richmond* (William Bertrand inventory), 76

Richier, Jeanne (Charlotte Bertrand's grandmother), 75

Robert* (William Ballandine inventory) 68

Roberts, Thomas* (servant of John Bertrand), 35

Robin* (man— Charles Ewell will and inventory), 68

Robin* (William Ballandine inventory), 68

Robinson, John, 120

Rose* (William Bertrand inventory), 76

Rose* (Thomas Bertrand Griffin inventory), 92

Roy, Elie, 124

Roy, Jeanne, 124

Roy, Judith, 124

Salkeld, Henry,* 51-52, 57

Salkeld, Mary Ann (nee Bertrand?), 52

Sam* (Thomas Bertrand Griffin inventory), 92

Sam* (Thomas Bertrand Griffin inventory), 92

Sampson* (William Bertrand inventory), 76

Sally* (Thomas Bertrand Griffin inventory), 92

Sarah* (Charles Ewell will and inventory), 68

Sarah* (William Bertrand inventory), 76

Sarah* (William Bertrand inventory), 76

Sarry* (girl— Charles Ewell inventory), 68

Seldon, _____, 121

Senex, John, 77

Servant, Jacques, 123

Smith, John (Captain), 2, 5

Sonny* (James Foushee will), 66

Stephenson, William* (servant of John Bertrand), 35

John Steptoe, 47

Stuart, Christina* (Lady), 85-86, 113, 120

Stuart, John (Sixth Earl of Traquair), 85-86, 113

Sue* (John Bertrand will), 35

Sue* (woman—Charles Ewell inventory), 68

Sue* (William Ballandine inventory), 68

Sukey* (girl—Charles Ewell inventory), 68

Suzis* (William Bertrand inventory), 76

Sydnor, William, 67

Taylor, _____, 121

Taylor, Eve (nee Ball), 70, 121

Tebbs, Charlotte (nee Foushee), 66

Tenney, Robert* (servant of Charlotte Bertrand), 46

Thibaud, Suzanne, 123

Thornton, Charles, 121

Thornton, Thomas (the Reverend), 121

Tom* (enslaved worker of John Bertrand), 35

Tom* (James Foushee will), 66

Tom* (William Bertrand inventory), 76

Tom* (William Bertrand inventory), 76

Tom* (Thomas Bertrand Griffin inventory), 55

Tomlyn, William, 21, 117

Toney* (man—Charles Ewell inventory), 68

Tourtellot, Abraham, 123

Tourtellot, Benjamin, 123

Tourtellot, Daniel, 123

Tourtellot, Jeanne, 123

Tourtellot, Louis (Sieur de la Souroc), 123

Tourtellot, Suzanne, 123

Tourtellot, Simon, 123

Trenace, _____, 121

Waddelow, Temperance, 58

Washington, George, 70, 101-102

Washington, Mary (nee Ball), 70

Webb, Sarah* (servant of John Kyrby), 22

Whitaker, Thomas* (servant of John Bertrand), 35

White, Isaac, Sr., 73, 121

White, Isaac, Jr., 121

White, Mary Ann* (nee Ewell), 73

Will* (William Bertrand inventory), 76

Will* (Thomas Bertrand Griffin inventory), 92

Will* (Thomas Bertrand Griffin inventory), 92

Winney* (William Bertrand inventory), 76

Winny* (Thomas Bertrand Griffin inventory), 92

Withinbrook, Thomas, 20, 25

Wormley, Mary, 103, 114

Wormley, Ralph IV, 103, 114

Young Betty* (Charles Ewell will and inventory), 68

Young Jack* (James Foushee will), 66

Young Tom* (James Foushee will), 66